4.00

Donated by -
St. Ambrose Christian Mothers

Please return to:
Aquinas Academy Library
2308 West Hardies Road
Gibsonia, PA 15044
724-444-0722

DISCARD

FRONTIER HERO
Simon Kenton

BORN: April 3, 1755
DIED: April 29, 1836

Simon Kenton was one of the truly outstanding figures of the early frontier. In the days when Kentucky and the Ohio territory were unmapped country where Indians prized a white man's scalp, Simon was known among the pioneers as a leader and guide in their struggle to wrest the land from the wilderness. Danger was his constant companion. He was captured by Indians, almost burned at the stake—but nothing could diminish his courage or lessen his faith in the American ideal. His action-packed story vividly brings to life the men and qualities of leadership displayed during the western movement in our history.

BOOKS BY SHANNON GARST

AMELIA EARHART: HEROINE OF THE SKIES
ANNIE OAKLEY
BIG FOOT WALLACE OF THE TEXAS RANGERS
BROKEN-HAND FITZPATRICK: GREATEST OF MOUNTAIN MEN
BUFFALO BILL
CHIEF JOSEPH OF THE NEZ PERCES
COWBOY-ARTIST: CHARLES M. RUSSELL
CUSTER: FIGHTER OF THE PLAINS
FRONTIER HERO: SIMON KENTON
JACK LONDON: MAGNET FOR ADVENTURE
JAMES BOWIE AND HIS FAMOUS KNIFE
JOE MEEK: MAN OF THE WEST
KIT CARSON: TRAIL BLAZER AND SCOUT
SCOTTY ALLAN: KING OF THE DOG-TEAM DRIVERS
SITTING BULL: CHAMPION OF HIS PEOPLE
THREE CONQUISTADORS: CORTEZ, CORONADO, PIZARRO
WILL ROGERS: IMMORTAL COWBOY

with Warren Garst

ERNEST THOMPSON SETON: NATURALIST
WILD BILL HICKOK

FRONTIER HERO
Simon Kenton

by Shannon Garst

92
K19

JULIAN MESSNER, INC.
New York

Published by Julian Messner, Inc.
8 West 40th Street, New York 18

Published simultaneously in Canada
by The Copp Clark Publishing Co. Limited

© Copyright 1963 by Doris Shannon Garst

Printed in the United States of America
Library of Congress Catalog Card No. 63—8643

For
EVELYN HINSON

Acknowledgments

This book is based on the biography, *Simon Kenton; His Life and Period, 1755–1836,* by Edna Kenton; on the sketch of Simon Kenton by John Alexander McClung, and also upon the sketch of Simon Kenton by John McDonald, which was published in the *Western Christian Advocate* in 1835. The Edna Kenton biography and the sketches were in turn based upon material collected by Lyman Copeland Draper, who intended to write a biography of Kenton, but his work was unpublished until others used it. Draper accumulated a mass of source material which is in the archives of the State Historical Library at Madison, Wisconsin. The two sketches mentioned above were also based upon the Draper collection, as is everything else that has been published about Simon Kenton.

My sincere thanks go to the staff of the Wisconsin State Historical Library for their courtesy and promptness in furnishing me with photostats of essential material. My thanks also to Mrs. Alys Freeze and her staff of the Western History Department of the Denver Public Library and to Laura Chambers of the Carnegie Library of Converse County, Wyoming. These two last-named patient and efficient librarians have a hand in nearly every biography I write.

SHANNON GARST

Contents

Acknowledgments   7
1   The Runaway   13
2   The Life of an Indian   39
3   In Seach of Kain-Tuck-Ee   42
4   Indian Troubles Increase   55
5   Troubled Times   68
6   Captured!   76
7   Dreams of Empire   95
8   Kenton and His "Boys"   110
9   Work Well Done   121
10   "On His Own Hook"   133
11   Trouble in the Settlements   142
12   Simon's Last War   152
13   Kentucky Returns A Favor   162
14   End of The Trail   173
     Bibliography   183
     Index   185

FRONTIER HERO

CHAPTER 1

The Runaway

The Kenton home at the foot of Bull Run Mountain, Virginia, was in a hubbub of excitement. Tomorrow the highlight of the year would begin—the "rolling" to market of the hogshead filled with nearly a thousand pounds of tightly packed tobacco. This was the family money crop which had to be taken to Dumfries forty miles away.

Fifteen-year-old Simon filled a poke—a hide sack—with jerky, the cured and dried meat of a deer. He himself had killed the animal, for Simon was the hunter of the family. Mark Kenton, his father, was hammering the lid on the hogshead while the older boys, Mark junior and John, nailed the crossbar and shafts for the horses in place. Mary, the mother, and the girls, Mary, Jane and Frances, were busy frying cornmeal journey cakes on a big iron skillet before the great fireplace. The little ones, Benjamin and Nancy, were too young to do anything but get in everyone's way.

The whole family went to bed early that night for they must be up at dawn the following day. But only Mr. Kenton, John, young Mark and Simon would make the journey.

By the time breakfast was over the next morning, the sun was peeping over the edge of the world. The older boys packed the sleeping robes and supplies on a horse, while Simon and his father hitched the team to the shafts of the big barrel.

"Gitty-ap," the father shouted.

The two horses strained against the harness and the great hogshead began to roll.

"We're off!" cried Simon as he thrust aloft the long rifle he was carrying. He would lead the little procession, while his keen eyes scanned the forest beside the trail for game.

He and his brothers and father were dressed alike in fringed buckskin breeches and linsey-woolsey shirts that came midway to their thighs. They had raised the flax on their own farm, and their mother had woven the cloth from which the long shirts were made. Each wore a belt which tied in back, and carried in it a hunting knife. Over the shoulder hung a strap to which was attached a powder horn—once grown on the head of a cow. The front of each shirt had a loose panel from the waist to the neck which served as a pocket. In it were stowed all sorts of odds and ends—pieces of journey cake, jerky, flint and steel, swabs for the rifle and other items that might come in handy. Hanging under the left arm from the strap was a pouch that held shot, patches and tinder.

By noon six other parties of barrel rollers had joined the Kentons, and it pleased Simon to see them. So many people would make a night of camping out under the stars a merry one. Also, it made him feel important to be leading such a grand procession. He whistled happily on that crisp, sunny day and took long strides to keep well in the lead.

Although he was alert in watching for game beside the road, he knew that there was little chance of his seeing any. The men and boys following him were making too much noise with their laughing, talking and shouting at their horses.

At fifteen, Simon was tall for his age and sturdy, and shooting up so fast that his breeches and shirt sleeves were always too short. He had blue eyes, copper-colored hair and a plentiful crop of freckles.

While the rollers stopped to graze their horses during the noon hour, a wagon drove up to where men and boys were eating lunch. Simon's heart beat fast when he saw the girl with whom he was in love. Ellen Cummins was seated between her mother and her father, her fair curls edging a blue sunbonnet which matched the color of her eyes.

Simon had fallen in love with Ellen during the rolling of the previous year and had worshipped her secretly from afar during church meetings, husking bees and other local social events. Her father was rolling a barrel of tobacco to Dumfries and was taking his wife and daughter with him. In town they would trade their tobacco and other farm products carried in his wagon for various supplies. A neighbor, nineteen-year-old William Leachman, had been hired to drive the team pulling the Cummins' hogshead.

Frontier Hero

All afternoon Simon hoped desperately to sight some game so that he could display his excellent shooting skill to Ellen. Then he imagined her father's team running away and he, Simon the hero, leaping in front and stopping the animals at risk of his life. But the team failed to run away, and not even a squirrel showed for him to bring down for his fair Ellen's supper.

At sundown the procession halted and the teams were unhitched, hobbled and turned loose to graze. Campfires blazed along the trail as the rollers prepared the evening meal. Simon, his father and his brothers ate a plain supper of jerky and journey cakes, but the Cummins were better supplied because of their wagon. They had a big iron kettle hung on a rod resting on two forked sticks over the fire, and from it came smells that made Simon's mouth water and the jerky he was chewing very tough and tasteless.

Loud talk and much laughter rang in the air around the camp as the members of the group visited back and forth. Simon wished that his father would go to the campfire of the Cummins family so that he would have an excuse to tag along and get closer to his dream maiden. He could not muster up enough nerve to go calling upon Ellen alone. Pretending not to look, he watched the Cummins' party fill trenchers from the big kettle and sat down to supper. To Simon's anguish he saw young William Leachman hand Ellen a trencher and wooden spoon and sit down beside her to eat.

Instantly Simon was devoured by jealousy. He had not noticed before how good-looking William Leachman was. Now as he saw William and Ellen talking and laughing

The Runaway

together, immense anger and hatred surged up in Simon's heart. Suddenly he detested everything about William—especially his long hair which he wore braided in a queue.

That night after supper there was singing around a central campfire, and Simon watched in jealous agony as William and Ellen joined the group. At first he pretended to sing along just to show how little he cared that the girl he loved seemed to be enjoying young Leachman's company. Then finding this too difficult to keep up, Simon withdrew to the edge of the crowd and brooded in silent misery.

The group broke up early to get some sleep, for everyone must be on the way at dawn. Mr. Kenton's camp was close to that of the Cummins family, and as Simon was about to bed down for the night on his bearskin, he saw in the moonlight two forms behind the Cummins' wagon. Ellen and William! As Simon saw Leachman about to kiss her a blind fury swept over him. Like a wild animal Simon rushed over and threw himself at William, punching him repeatedly in a mad rage. Leachman fell back in surprise under the assault but soon rallied and fought back strongly. Being older and larger he finally knocked Simon to the ground, sat on his stomach and held the younger boy's shoulders down as he struggled desperately to get up.

Ellen's screams had alerted the whole camp, and all of the rollers rushed over to see what was going on.

"You little fool," William growled, "what got into you?"

"You insulted Ellen. You were trying to force your attentions on her."

Frontier Hero

"I was about to kiss the girl I'm going to marry," Leachman explained. "We're engaged."

Simon wished the earth would open and swallow him. He had lost Ellen and been made to look ridiculous in front of her and all these people.

Then to make his humiliation complete, William helped him to his feet as he would a small boy. "Come on now. Let's be friends you young wildcat." He gave Simon a couple of playful jabs on the chin. With this bitter salt rubbed into his wounds, Simon's anger flamed anew, and he charged into William flailing wildly with his fists. Immediately his brothers leaped in and pulled the two apart.

The next day a badly swollen black eye and a bruised cheekbone were ample evidence of Simon's defeat. It was difficult for him to face the others—but especially Ellen. Yet face her he must, for she came to meet him as he was putting his rolled-up bearskin on a horse.

"I'm—I'm sorry about last night," she said hesitantly. "It was good of you to try to protect me."

"I made a fool of myself," Simon muttered. "But I didn't mean to embarrass you."

"You had no way of knowing that we were engaged," she said softly. "We haven't been for very long."

Simon's love for Ellen was only increased by her sweet concern. And as his love for her grew so did his wild hatred of young Leachman, whom he saw blindly as his enemy. But for the rest of the rolling trip he remained silent and withdrawn.

That night they camped outside of Dumfries, for they were all tenant farmers and could not afford to stay at the

The Runaway

tavern. The next morning they rolled the barrels to the store where the tobacco was tallied and paid for, and Mr. Graham, who owned the land that these farmers leased, collected his rents. After the rent was paid, what supplies were needed were bought at the same store, the purchases being mainly tools, ammunition and lengths of calico for the women to make dresses and sunbonnets. Then as soon as the buying was done, the party set out to roll the barrels back on the home journey.

Simon was still subdued. What had started as a high adventure had turned out to be a bitter humiliation to him. Yet, though he was a very sad and chastened boy, as he strode along he fiercely vowed to himself that somehow, someday, he would even the score with William Leachman. He would work and train until his muscles were strong, and be ready for the day of reckoning which must come eventually.

The Kenton home in Fauquier County, Virginia, was set in a fertile valley at the foot of Bull Run Mountain. There Mark Kenton, who had come from Ireland, brought his wife, the former Mary Miller, a young woman of Scotch-Welsh descent. There the couple built their log cabin and reared their brood of eight children. Simon was born April 3, 1755, the seventh in line.

William, the oldest son, was married and established as a tenant farmer a few miles away from the home place. He and Mark junior were the only ones of the family who had gone to school.

The father had said one day during the evening meal,

"I'll do my best to educate any of you young'uns who will work hard at his book learning. But it costs me two dollars a month for each of you who goes to school, and I'm a poor man. I can't afford to educate any of you who isn't eager to learn."

Simon spoke up, "I went to school for half a day, and that was enough for me. I couldn't sit still that long."

"You'll have to be a farmer then," his father pointed out. "There isn't anything else for a poor, uneducated man to do."

"William went to school for all eight grades," Simon grinned, "and he's a tenant farmer. I don't see what good all that book learning did him."

"William likes farming," Mr. Kenton went on, "and he's the hardest working of any of you."

Simon said, "I hate farming—stooping over to plant seed, plowing with a wooden plow. All that hoeing and everything. But I learn a lot when I'm out in the woods—all about plants and trees and things that grow wild, and about animals. I reckon I'll make my living by being a hunter."

"Well," his father said, pushing away the wooden trencher that had held his food, "I'll have to say that you're a good hunter. You've kept us supplied with meat ever since I taught you to use my rifle. Even before that you used to bring in small game you shot with your bow and arrow." He smiled and added, "You are a natural-born woodsman."

Simon would do the daily chores willingly enough, such as chopping and bringing in wood and pounding hominy.

The Runaway

But he was exceptionally clever at trapping, hunting and skinning game of all kinds. Unable to read or write, he was self-reliant and wise in the ways of nature. He knew the calls of each kind of bird and could track animals with an uncanny instinct.

He learned to throw the tomahawk and practiced this skill faithfully, also the rapid loading and accurate firing of his father's long rifle. He loved roaming the wilds, and no hunt was too hard nor the weather so fierce it could stop him. But he detested the drudgery of farm work—the backbreaking job of planting, the never-ending hoeing. As there were plenty of others to do the farm work, he spent most of his time in the woods, an arrangement which proved to be best for everyone. The Kentons always had a larger supply of game meat on hand than anyone in the valley.

Simon had just turned sixteen when his father sent him over to the Leachman farm to borrow the long saw that was neighborhood property.

His heart suddenly beat faster as he set out on the errand. For months he had nursed his wounded pride and jealousy until he could scarcely hide the sullen hatred within him. Now he was a little heavier, taller and stronger than the night he had been beaten and shamed by William Leachman. Simon had been waiting a long time to settle the score with his enemy, and this might be his chance.

He found the senior Mr. Leachman behind the house building a shed and William just coming in from the woods with an armload of shingles.

Frontier Hero

"My father sent me to borrow the neighborhood saw," Simon said.

"It's back in the woods where William's been working," said Mr. Leachman. "We're through with it and you're welcome to it. Will, show Simon where it is."

"Sure," William agreed and dumped the load of shingles near his father. "Come on, Simon. The saw is stashed out here a piece." He grinned in a friendly way as he swung off into the woods.

Simon followed grimly, waiting until they got well out of sight and hearing of the father, and then called sharply to William, "Hold it!"

Young Leachman turned around in surprise as Simon snapped, "Get 'em up. This time I'm going to beat the smartness out of you and knock that silly smile off your face for good."

Simon stepped in quickly and rocked William with four or five blows that sent him reeling back bleeding from the mouth. As Simon rushed forward again, young Leachman ducked down and grabbed him around the arms, holding on a moment until his head cleared. Then abruptly he released him and smashed a fist up against the side of Simon's jaw that turned him half-around, and he went down.

As in their previous fight, once again Simon found himself on his back, staring up into the face of his hated tormentor. He knew now he was no match for his stronger foe but would not admit defeat. Suddenly he saw a chance and with one convulsive heave got William off. Springing up Simon darted back of him and seized his hair queue.

The Runaway

With a quick yank back he knotted the braid to a sturdy sapling tree.

He attacked young Leachman and beat him unconscious before he could free his queue. And as his enemy sank inert to the ground, Simon stood over him gasping for breath.

Suddenly his sense of triumph was swept away as fear entered Simon's heart. His fallen foe had not moved. He had not even groaned. Worried now, he tried to prop William against the tree, but Leachman sagged limply to the ground. He wiped the blood from William's face with his fingers and cleaned them on the grass. He could see no sign of breathing and the horrible thought dawned on him that he had killed William.

In a panic Simon turned and started to run toward home. Then he stopped short as he realized that he could not return there—ever! Mr. Leachman had seen them going into the forest. Before long he would find his son's body and know that Simon was the murderer. With a groan of despair he took off wildly into the woods and ran as long as he had breath to do so. Finally exhausted, he hid underneath some bushes. His shirt and linsey-woolsey breeches were smeared with blood, and after resting awhile he found a stream and tried to remove the signs of his crime with water-soaked leaves.

Then he ran on until he came to a forest trail which he followed until he was again out of breath, and once more he hid in some bushes. He rejected the terrible yearning he had to get up and retrace his steps. The homeward pull was strong—but he was certain that by now he was a hunted criminal. He could never go back. Oh, why had

Frontier Hero

he allowed his passion to get the best of him and lead him to commit murder!

Simon took to the trail again and ran until evening, when hunger and fatigue stopped him. He found and ate several edible plants and a few berries, but they did little to sustain him. Still worn out and hungry, as darkness came he went off into some bushes and stretched out on the ground. But he slept little the whole night, ridden by his guilt and sorrow.

He traveled on and spent another miserable night in the woods. On the second day he came up to three men who were making a clearing in the forest.

"Can you give me a job?" he asked the oldest—a giant of a man with black hair and beard.

"I haven't any money to pay you," the man replied.

"I'll work if you'll feed me," Simon said.

"Fair enough," the man agreed. "You a runaway?"

"No," Simon lied. "I'm out to make my fortune. I haven't any family. My parents are dead."

All three of the men looked at him curiously, but went on with their work when the big one set him to sawing down a tree. Simon worked until he grew faint with hunger, then finally gained enough courage to say, "I haven't had anything to eat since the day before yesterday except roots and berries."

"Then you must be starved," the leader grunted. He pointed to a rude lean-to shelter on the edge of the clearing. "You'll find some rabbit stew simmering in that pot on the fire. Help yourself."

Simon worked at the clearing all day, and that night he

The Runaway

slept beneath the lean-to. At breakfast the next morning the big man told him that he was welcome to stay and work for his meals.

"Thank you," Simon said, "but I've got to find a job to earn money for a gun. With a rifle I could feed myself. I'm a good hunter."

Simon said good-by and continued along the trail until near evening, when he came to a cabin where two children were playing. As their mother saw him approach she called the children inside and barred the door.

"Please, ma'am," he called out, "I mean no harm. And I'm mighty hungry. I haven't eaten anything since sun-up."

"Go see my husband. He's working down in the fields."

Simon walked on until he came to a cornfield where a man was hoeing.

"I'll help you with your work," he said. "I don't ask money. Just some food."

The man agreed and let him sleep in the barn. He worked there for two days before again pushing on to look for a place where he could earn money.

He followed the trail to the Cheat Valley region, living on roots and berries when there were no settlers for whom to work for his board. At some of the cabins people treated him with suspicion, obviously thinking he was at least a runaway, or worse, a criminal.

One day an idea struck him. He could avoid such suspicion and gain instant acceptance by claiming to be distant kin to the settlers. All he had to do was learn who lived a day's journey ahead of him on the trail. If that man

Frontier Hero

was named "Brown," Simon was a "Brown" from another area. If his name was "Smith," Simon's was "Smith." Thus he changed his name daily and was shown frontier hospitality in every cabin where he stopped.

Then he reached the farm of a man named Butler, who was so kind that Simon decided to accept the good job his new-found "relative" offered him. This man had a flour mill as well as a farm, and Simon stayed until he finally earned enough to buy a gun. Since he had gotten acquainted with a number of people while he worked for Butler and was known widely by that name, he decided to use permanently the name "Simon Butler."

One day a man named Daniel Johnson came to the farm. "I'm a native of the state of New Jersey," he said, "on a journey to see the country, but with no destination in view."

"I've been working here for some time," Simon told him, "but my feet are beginning to itch to be on the trail again."

"Then come with me," Johnson said. "I have supplies that will, with the game we kill, be enough for both of us."

So the two went along the trail together to Warm Springs, then northward into the Allegheny wilderness. Game was plentiful and Simon did not have to go to sleep hungry, beg or work for food, or change his name as a trick to win hospitality.

He and Johnson parted when they reached Ice's Ford, near the junction of the Monongahela and the Cheat rivers. Simon worked there for a while to earn enough money to

The Runaway

replace his worn-out clothes and buy more powder and lead. There he met and joined four men—John and Joe Mahon, William Grille and Jacob Greathouse—who were about to set out on a hunting trip.

He helped them hollow out a canoe from a great log, by burning and scraping out the center, and in this they descended the Monongahela until they reached Provence settlement near Fort Pitt. There they met an Indian trader who told the Mahons that their father, who had recently been captured by Indians, was still alive and a prisoner at Fort Pitt. The hunting trip was given up as the Mahon brothers set out in search of their father.

Simon stayed on in Provence settlement, working whenever he could find a job, until he had acquired new deerskin pants, moccasins and a hunting shirt. Then he met John Yeager and young George Strader. Simon took an instant liking to the older man, who always had a tale to tell of high adventure. As a child Yeager had been captured by Indians and had lived with them until he was a young man. He could speak their language, knew their customs and had gone on many of their big hunts. But the marvel of all was when he told about the wonderful land through which he had wandered.

"The Kain-tuck-ee cane lands are the most beautiful on earth," Yeager told Simon. "The soil is the richest, everything grows better there, and game is thicker than you could dream. It is a paradise on earth, and all free land! Anyone could settle there, and living on the country would be easy."

Frontier Hero

"That's the place I'm looking for," Simon said eagerly. "Could you lead me there?"

Yeager hesitated. "It's been many years since I crossed that country with the Injuns. I was only a boy then." Then he brightened. "But I think I can find it. If we get to the Ohio and go down it for a few days we'd reach the old Injun crossing. I'd know it by the cane lands that border the southern shore. That land is different from any other place on earth."

"I'd like to go there!" Simon cried.

"You say there's lots of game?" young Strader asked.

"All you want. Herds of buffalo, deer, elk, and the streams are rich with beaver."

Simon thought aloud. "We could get rich by hunting and trapping. Hoard our furs and canoe them up the Ohio once a year. What a way to make a living!"

The two boys were fired with enthusiasm. They must go without delay to this wonderful land of Kain-tuck-ee and build a camp. Yeager would tend it, do the cooking and tan the hides, while the boys hunted and trapped.

They made a log canoe and loaded it with blankets, rifles, ammunition, traps, ground corn, and salt. Later they would make coonskin hats for winter cold. Now they wore gaudy bandannas on their heads, to keep their hair from getting caught in brambles. As they pushed off down the Monongahela for Fort Pitt, Simon looked over his shoulder. The small stockade of Provence faded in the morning mist and a lump came into his throat. He missed his folks and was sorry he had grieved them. Though each day he grew a little more numb to the past, he had to swallow that lump several times now. Would he ever see his family again?

Simon set his shoulders determinedly and faced forward. There was only one way now for him to look—ahead.

CHAPTER 2

The Life of an Indian

A feeling of high adventure began to rise in Simon as the three floated downriver. Eighteen miles later they came to Logstown, a Shawnee village where John Gibson kept a small trading post, and lingered there for a few days. The Shawnee were then at peace with the white man and made the strangers welcome. Simon listened carefully to the talk around him, and his keen young mind quickly picked up snatches of the Indian tongue. When his party again set out in the canoe, he was at Yeager constantly to teach him Indian words and phrases. He had a feeling that someday he might have use for this knowledge.

At Yellow Creek they came abreast of the camp of the Mingo chief, Logan.

"Let's stop here," Simon suggested eagerly. "I want to meet the chief."

"We haven't the time to waste," Yeager pointed out. "We must get to the cane lands, set up our traps and start laying in a stock of furs."

Seventy miles from Fort Pitt they pulled their canoe

The Life of an Indian

ashore and hid it in the brush; then they followed a trail which Yeager said would lead them to a town of friendly Mingoes. They were welcomed by the natives and stayed in the village for three days, eating with the Indians and taking part in their dances.

As they prepared to leave, Simon said, "Maybe the Indians have the right idea about the way to live. We call them savages. But in some ways they are happier than us whites. We're always trying to make more money and buy more things which just clutter up our lives."

Yeager pointed to a small stream which entered the river there. "That," he explained, "is Big Grave Creek. And that mound beside it is where Indians are buried who died fighting for their land."

Near Kanawha they stopped for three days with a band of friendly Delawares. The three adventurers were by now almost like Indians themselves, and they fished, swam, ate and danced with the natives. Simon was delighted to find that he now could speak and understand some of both their sign language and their spoken one.

Simon studied the ways of Indians and how they moved through the forest as silently as shadows, seeming to blend in with their surroundings. Like them, he trained his mind to send out "feelers" that would warn him of danger or anything unusual. He learned also to "read signs," those faint traces left by the passing of an animal or an enemy— a turned blade of grass, a fallen leaf pressed into the ground, a dim footprint.

He trained himself to walk as they did, with his eyes generally looking down, but with quick glances all around

Frontier Hero

which took in every detail. These skills would remain with him all of his life, and constant alertness would save his life many a time.

They took off in the canoe again, but Yeager's "few days" had lengthened into weeks. Still they had not come to the cane lands and Simon began to believe that Kentucky existed only in the man's imagination. However, the country was beautiful. Indian summer lay over the land, and the willows, scrub oak, maples and sycamores were changing into vivid colors.

They passed many islands, all inviting and mysterious. Then they floated past the awe-inspiring Ohio palisades, which rose sheerly toward the heavens, shutting the sun's rays off from the river. Soon the stream began to run dangerously swift, and it took all of the skill of the three oarsmen to keep the canoe from overturning. When they shot over the rapids of Letart's Falls, Simon's heart was in his throat. He was sure that they would capsize.

"This is the Big Sandy," Yeager said, as they passed the mouth of a gushing river. "From now on we are in Kentucky."

"But where are the canebrakes?" Simon asked.

Yeager shrugged. "Inland, I guess. But isn't this country to suit your taste?"

"It's wonderful," Simon admitted. "So why not pick out a likely campsite and settle down before winter sets in?"

"That's a good idea," Strader agreed.

Yeager frowned. "Seems we should have come to the

[32]

The Life of an Indian

canebrakes before this. Maybe we passed them. Let's turn back and explore the south shore again."

They stopped at various places and traveled inland for some distance, but could not find the canebrakes. Finally they reached the mouth of the Great Kanawha, turned the prow of their canoe upstream and followed it to the mouth of Elk River.

"There's a big trail that leads off along the Kanawha here!" Simon cried in excitement.

"It's a buffalo run," Yeager said after looking it over.

Following the rutted trail, broad as a wagon road, they found it led to a salt spring.

"The perfect place for a camp!" Yeager exclaimed. "Near enough to the Ohio River to transport our furs or reach in time of danger. And far enough from unfriendly Indians passing up and down it."

"And," Simon added, "being so close to this game trail will supply us with food and furs."

Yeager directed the building of their camp. They used a huge fallen tree for the back of their cabin and cleared the brush and grass from a square in front of it. Then they stomped this earth into a hard flooring and at the front of the square set up two forked poles. A stout pole was set in the forks and other poles laid at right angles on it over to the tree trunk. On this foundation for a roof they piled brush and sod. The sides were built with logs and chinked with clay and moss.

Before the open face of their cabin they piled rocks to make a crude fireplace for cooking and warmth. At night, wrapped in blankets and fur robes, they slept on beds of grass and moss with their feet to the fire.

During that first winter they lived like Indians, which Simon considered an ideal way. He and Strader did most of the hunting while Yeager tended camp and helped tan the hides.

There were times when Simon thought of his family, and homesickness saddened him, but these became less frequent. There was so much to do that he had little time to brood, and his campmates were good company. Besides, their stock of pelts was piling up and he was sure that their season of trapping and hunting would yield a good profit.

When spring came they piled their furs in the canoe, paddled down to the Ohio and waited at the mouth of the Kanawha for some passing trader. Finally one came by in a large canoe, stocked with a good supply of corn, clothing, guns, ammunition and even luxuries such as coffee and brown sugar. The three adventurers spent an entire day in trading, and during that time were told the news of the frontier.

"A few settlers," the trader concluded, "are drifting in; but the country will remain a wilderness and hunters' paradise for a long time."

They lived another year safely in their snug camp; but contrary to what the trader had said, in March of 1773 the inevitable happened. So far they had not seen an Indian, friendly or hostile. Then one cold, rainy day Strader and Kenton went out to tend their traps, and on the way back Simon shot a young turkey. While it cooked over the blaze that Yeager had ready, the two young men carefully

The Life of an Indian

wiped their guns dry, wrapped them in blankets and set them in the back of their cabin. Then seated on a log in front, they took off their moccasins and leggings to allow them to dry before the fire.

Yeager was standing beside the fire turning the roasting turkey on a rifle ramrod, the blaze clearly outlining him. A slight, unusual sound caused Simon to look up quickly. The same sound attracted the notice of all three. Simon's heart nearly stopped beating when he saw half a dozen Indians a short distance away, their rifles leveled.

Kenton and Strader sprang to their feet.

"Meet you at rendezvous one!" Simon shouted and took off at top speed. He meant that they should join up at the first of two places chosen in advance for just such a crisis. If rendezvous one was in danger, they would meet at number two. All frontiersmen, in constant danger of attack, arranged such details beforehand.

As he ran Simon heard shots, and quickly glancing back saw Yeager stumble toward the Indians. He was either wounded or trying to speak to the Indians who were closing in on him with their tomahawks upraised.

Late that night Simon and Strader met at Yellow Creek, both winded from running and famished for food. They had no clothes but the shirts on their backs. They were without guns, leggings or moccasins.

"Maybe we ought to go back and see what happened to poor Yeager," Simon suggested.

"I can tell you what happened to him," Strader said grimly. "I looked back and saw an Indian swing his tomahawk down on our friend's head. His scalp is now dangling

Frontier Hero

at some warrior's belt. If we go back, they'll get ours too."

Horror froze Simon's blood in his veins. "Maybe," he suggested weakly, "they didn't actually kill Yeager."

"I saw them," Strader insisted tersely. "Our friend is dead. We couldn't do him any good by going back. We'd only endanger ourselves."

"They'll follow us," Simon said tautly.

Strader nodded. "As soon as they divide the loot in our camp. So we'd better get going. Their yen for blood is aroused and they'll want to add our scalps to their collection."

Simon hesitated, thinking of Yeager.

"Come on!" Strader said impatiently. "Don't be a fool. Yeager is dead. We will be, too, if we don't get away from here."

They set out at a dogtrot toward the Ohio. When they were exhausted they left the trail and stretched out, cold and miserable on the wet ground.

For three days they traveled, guided by the sun or the moss on the trees, which they knew grew longer on the north side. By this time their strength was failing so alarmingly from lack of food that they could hardly stand. Then their feet got so swollen and sore from cuts and bruises that they could no longer walk. Forced to crawl, their knees and legs became raw and torn from briars and rocks.

"We'll never make it," Strader gasped as they stopped to rest. "Might as well lie here and stop struggling."

Simon said sternly, "You can't give up. We must go on." Much of the time they spent lying on the ground waiting

The Life of an Indian

to recover some strength, but when they were able to move, they could only push on a few yards.

Finally, in late afternoon of the fifth day they came to a trail. Simon gasped. "Maybe this leads to a cabin...."

"But which way? Left or right?" Strader groaned. "If we go wrong now, we're finished."

It was a vital question, and nothing about the path indicated the correct answer. But already Simon had developed that extra sense which would guide him the rest of his life.

"We go right," he said with certainty.

By nightfall they made their way to a small cabin. The owner, Amos Jones, kindly took them in and furnished them with homespun breeches and moccasins. Simon and Strader were more than grateful, for they could see by the surroundings that the settler was poor and had little clothing to spare.

While they were being clothed, the settler's wife pushed the stewpot close to the fire.

"I can see that you are nearly starved," she said.

"Don't bother to warm the stew," Strader begged in a cracked voice. "We'll eat it cold."

"No," she insisted. "It will take only a few minutes and will be better for you warm. And you must eat only a small bit at a time. How long since you have had food?"

"Five days," Simon told her.

Wet, clean cloths were provided to bathe and bind their feet while they waited for the stew to warm. Then she gave each a small amount of food in a bowl along with a thin slice of corn bread. They gulped the food in a moment and held out their bowls for more.

Frontier Hero

"No more now," she said firmly. "In an hour you can have a little more. If you eat as much as you'd like to right now it might kill you."

"Martha is right," Amos Jones agreed.

They remained at the kindly settler's cabin for four days, recovering their strength and waiting for their feet to heal enough so that they could walk. During this time Simon felt again the pangs of homesickness and sorrow. The crude cabin here reminded him of the snug, larger log dwelling where he had spent his happy boyhood.

What did the future hold for him? It looked very bleak. He could not go home. He had hoped to make a small fortune with his furs and send some of the money to help out his family. But in a few savage moments the fruits of a winter's work had been snatched away and one of his companions was dead. Now which way would the trail turn?

When Strader and Simon recovered, they set off along the Kanawha to the Ohio. Here they were lucky enough to find seven canoe loads of explorers commanded by Joel Reese. Simon was delighted to find among the men his friends, John and Joe Mahon, whom he had met two years ago at Ice's Ford.

Shaking hands with John, Simon asked, "Did you find your father?"

"Yes," John replied, "we found him at Fort Pitt. The Indians allowed him to be ransomed by the settlers."

Simon told him what he had been doing the past two years. "Then they scalped our companion, Yeager, and stole our furs and supplies," he finished.

The Life of an Indian

Reese frowned. "If the redskins are in a scalping mood, we will have to change our plans. Instead of going farther down the Ohio, we'll push on up to the mouth of the Little Kanawha. Dr. Briscoe is starting a settlement there, and we'll join him." Simon worked as a hunter for the settlement until May to pay off his borrowed rifle and buy a quantity of ammunition.

Strader went back to the Virginia settlements, and when he left it made Simon think of home. He yearned to visit his family, but dared not. Besides, no doubt by now they had disowned him because of his crime.

Several exploring parties were then at the mouth of the Great Kanawha, and all of them wanted him to join them because of his experience in the wilderness. He chose to go with the one under the command of Dr. John Wood, in which there were fourteen members. On the mouth of the Sandy they set up camp, and explorations continued out from that base.

On a trip down the Ohio, near Three Islands they saw ahead of them several canoes full of Indians, their faces daubed black and white with war paint. Before the hostiles saw them, Simon gave the signal for the explorers to pull quickly for the shore. Then moving quietly they hid their canoes in the bushes.

"What do we do now?" Dr. Wood whispered to Simon.

Kenton replied softly, "We'd best head overland to Virginia. It's our only chance."

"Can you guide us?" the doctor asked.

Simon nodded.

He led off silently, the others following, putting their

Frontier Hero

trust in an eighteen-year-old boy who had never been over this part of the wilderness before. Neither had any other white man ever set foot in this area.

It was a long, hard journey; game was scarce and hunger was a constant burden. They eked out their living with wild onions and other roots, and now and then Simon found a nest of turkey eggs.

One day as he was leading the group, Simon heard Dr. Wood just behind him utter a cry of pain. Simon whirled around thinking the doctor had been hit by an Indian arrow. But a copperhead snake which had bitten the doctor on the leg still lay coiled menacingly at his feet. Kenton shot it through the head and rushed up. Dr. Wood sat down, drew out his knife and gashed the snake-bite area on his leg, then used his neckerchief for a tourniquet. Simon knelt, put his mouth to the wound and sucked out the venom and spat it on the ground.

"I owe you a deep debt of gratitude. You saved my life," Dr. Wood told Simon.

Nevertheless Dr. Wood was very ill for two weeks and his leg swelled terribly. While the party laid over and waited for him to recover, Simon hunted each day and managed to bring in some game to eat. There was enough meat left over to cut into thin strips and dry on wooden frames over the campfire; and this jerky served to feed them on the remainder of the journey.

By some miracle Simon brought his party safely through the unfamiliar wilderness to Greenbriar County, an area of scattered settlements.

Simon's home was nearby and he longed to visit his fam-

[40]

ily's cabin during the night, but it was too close to the feared arm of the law.

He said good-by to his comrades of the danger trail and made his way alone back to the Monongahela country. Here he met again with his old friends the Mahon brothers and also with two adventurers, Greathouse and Grille. They were setting out on a hunting and trapping expedition and invited Simon to join them. While they were still building their canoe, Samuel Cartwright and Joseph Lock arrived and were invited to come along. Then the party of seven floated down the river until they came to the cabins which Dr. Wood's company had built near the Big Sandy. Simon was happy with his companions as they settled down to hunt and trap through the winter and into the spring of 1774.

CHAPTER 3

In Search of Kain-Tuck-Ee

News was slow in reaching the camp of Simon Kenton and his friends on the Big Sandy, but now and then a trader or settlers looking for new land came along. They told about increasing Indian danger on the frontier and recounted numerous attacks on settlements and frontier farms by savage hostiles.

"Where did these attacks take place?" Simon burst out, worried now about the safety of his family. "Have there been any attacks near Bull Run Mountain in Virginia?"

He was somewhat relieved to hear that the Indians had struck only the new border settlements. His kinfolks were safe; it was the new encroachments of white people along the Ohio that the Indians were resisting. Simon also heard rumors that the British were deliberately inciting the Indians to make trouble.

Then a trader came into camp with the terrible news that the entire family of Chief Logan of the Mingoes had been slain by white men.

"No!" Simon cried out in horror. "Logan was a fine

In Search of Kain-Tuck-Ee

man—a good friend of the whites. This senseless slaughter will make him our enemy, and God only knows how many innocent men, women and children will be slain in revenge."

The trader went on. "It may have been done to rile the Indians, so that the whites will have an excuse to drive them from the land. Some say Lord Dunmore, governor of Virginia, is deliberately stirring up these Indian troubles."

"Completely senseless," Simon said. "But what is this we hear about the thirteen colonies discussing independence from Great Britain?"

"It's true," the trader said, "and it's the real reason the redskins are on the warpath. The British are making allies of the Indians by supplying them with guns and ammunition, and are paying them for colonist scalps."

Simon shook his head over the serious news, and after the trader left, he and his companions discussed what they should do.

Simon said, "With the slaughter of Logan's family, we whites lost our best Injun friend. Now he and the Mingoes will stir up other tribes to help him get revenge. A small handful like us, all alone, could do little. So I think we should go to Fort Pitt and join up with our countrymen."

His friends agreed, and along the way they found the new settlers' cabins all deserted. "It's plain," Simon said, "that the occupants feared Logan's vengeance."

They arrived in May at Fort Pitt (later Pittsburgh) where they found many settlers and frontiersmen gathered. One of them, a tall, red-haired man, stepped forward and introduced himself. "I'm George Rogers Clark," he said, extending his hand and seizing Simon's in a firm grip.

Clark had a magnetic personality, and Simon felt himself instantly drawn to the man. Here, he felt, was a natural-born leader—one he could trust and follow.

"My name is Simon Butler," he said with a grin.

The same day that he met George Rogers Clark—the man who would become his personal hero as well as the hero of the frontier—Simon spotted a swarthy-skinned, dark-haired man who seemed to seek the shadows of the crowd. There was a sullen, brooding look of mystery about the stranger which aroused his curiosity, and finally Simon sought him out and introduced himself.

"My name's Simon, too," the man said. "Simon Girty."

After they had talked for a while, Girty spoke more freely.

"I was captured by the Injuns when I was a boy and I've lived among 'em for eight years. I reckon someways I'm more Injun than white. I feel strange among my own people now. If we weren't at war with the redskins, I'd go back to live with 'em again. I'd feel more at home."

"You don't side with the Indians against the whites!" Simon exclaimed.

"I've signed as a 'Britoner,' " Girty said abruptly. "I'm ready to use my knowledge of the country for the benefit of the whites."

Kenton grinned. "I too signed up as a Britoner, just this morning. Since we both have taken the oath of allegiance and are soldiers now, I hope we can be friends."

In Search of Kain-Tuck-Ee

Girty looked surprised, then pleased. "Thanks," he said. "I'm not one who makes friends easily."

Simon got his first military experience on McDonald's campaign against the Muskingum Indians. Four hundred men assembled at Wheeling and traveled downriver in boats to Captina, where they began their march inland. His skills in the wilderness were already widely known, so Simon was appointed to scout ahead of the army the places where the Indians could be found.

Clark was with this army and immediately showed his gift for leadership, which led Simon to admire him greatly. It was Clark also who clarified for him the reason why Lord Dunmore, governor of Virginia, had started the war against the Indians. It was done to divert the attention of the colonists from the British, because the American War of Independence was about to start.

Simon was somewhat puzzled. He knew that he must side with the settlers against the Indians, for the red man had wrought frightful havoc along the frontier. Their burning of settlements, scalping and other hideous methods of torture left no doubt in his mind that the Indians must be subdued. Yet he could understand their resentment against the white men who took their lands, laid bare their forests and killed off their game. But perhaps, he thought, the Indians should be willing to share it peacefully with the white men. The whites wanted to cultivate the soil, build homes and bring civilization to this fair country. When you came right down to it, he concluded, there was enough land for all.

From Captina, Simon led the march through ninety

Frontier Hero

miles of dense forest. It was his first experience in Ohio, but that sixth sense which he had developed since he began living in the wilderness enabled him to lead the way. It was as though his mind put out feelers and gave him a prevision of what lay ahead.

One day, without knowing how he knew it, he sensed that they were nearing a large Indian camp. Stopping in his tracks he held up his hands in the signal for the Britoners to prepare for an attack.

The men had just time enough to ready their rifles before a horde of howling, painted savages rushed out on them from the forest. Two white men were killed and several wounded, but the army was spared greater casualties because of Simon's alertness.

The hostiles fled after heavy losses, and by the time the soldiers reached the Indian village it was deserted. But Simon spotted a number of warriors hiding on the opposite shore of the stream, waiting to ambush the army as it crossed over. A flanking movement was begun, and when the Muskingums saw this they melted away into the forest. McDonald marched on along the Muskingum River, burning all the redskin villages and destroying their crops.

Simon so distinguished himself in this early campaign that McDonald, George Rogers Clark and Lord Dunmore all commended him. In addition, Dunmore appointed the nineteen-year-old lad to serve as scout along with Clark, Girty, Cresap and other highly experienced men.

Simon was a member of a ragtag and bobtail army, each individual a fine fighter, but none of them used to military discipline. As settlers they had dared danger and death to

In Search of Kain-Tuck-Ee

hew out their homes on the raw frontier, and they were a hardy lot. But no one, not even the officers, wore uniforms. Most of them were dressed in coarse breeches of linsey-woolsey, deerskin hunting shirts and crude caps of wool or fur. Each man furnished his own gun, tomahawk and scalping knife. And each furnished his own horse, or walked.

They hacked out their own roads as they traveled, drove their own cattle for meat or lived off the land. Pack horses carried their flour, salt and cornmeal, if they were lucky enough to have such supples. When they came to a river that had to be navigated, they cut down trees and built their canoes. It took them five weeks to travel to the Elk River, a distance of 160 miles. By that time they were a seasoned army that knew how to push its way through the wilderness. They fought and won the battle of Point Pleasant. And though it was fought for the British Crown, in effect it was the first battle of the Revolution. The courageous victory there gave the colonists pride and confidence in the fighting abilities of their frontiersmen.

While serving in Dunmore's army, Simon with two other men was sent to Lowther's Fort on the West Fork of the Monongahela. He was carrying secret dispatches to Captain Lewis, and on the way they were attacked by Indians. The three messengers ran, as planned before in case of trouble, in different directions. When he felt that he had gotten safely away Simon tried to find his companions, but failing to do so he continued on his way alone.

Captain Lewis did not believe Simon's story. It was inconceivable to the officer that this young lad could have made such a dangerous trip alone, and he suspected that

Frontier Hero

Simon was an enemy spy. Lewis sent messengers back to Dunmore's army to find out the truth, and until they returned and cleared him, Simon was held prisoner.

Freed, and in good standing, Simon made his way alone back to Fort Pitt. By now he was wishing he had a companion to share his dangerous work. Simon Girty would make a good partner, he thought. After that he was sent back and forth twice more to Captain Lewis with important messages, and Girty went with him on those two trips. They became kindred spirits in the quiet forest, facing the perils of death. As Kenton later wrote, "Girty and I, two lonely men on the banks of the Ohio, pledged ourselves one to the other, hand in hand, for life or death, when there was nobody in the wilderness but God and us."

As they journeyed together Girty again told Simon, but in more detail, how he had been captured as a boy by the Senecas and of his life among them for eight years. Surrendered later to the English, Girty had served them as an interpreter until the time he met Simon.

Simon, Girty and a settler called McCulloch were sent by Lord Dunmore with orders for Lewis to join him on the Ohio side.

"Is the man mad!" Lewis raged. "My soldiers are exhausted and our stockades are not built. To abandon this place now would leave the Virginia frontier wide open to the savages. Tell Dunmore we refuse to comply with his order."

Simon and his two friends returned to Fort Pitt with the message, and in doing so they missed the one big battle of the Dunmore War. Early the next morning Chief Corn-

In Search of Kain-Tuck-Ee

stalk with a thousand Shawnee attacked Lewis and his force at Point Pleasant. Lewis decisively beat them, putting an end to the Dunmore War, and the Indians soon sued for peace.

At Camp Charlotte where the treaty ending the Dunmore War was signed, Simon met another man who would play an important part in his life—Logan, the famed Mingo chief. After Lord Dunmore stated the terms of peace, Simon saw Logan walk with dignity to the great elm tree beneath which the treaty-makers sat in a circle.

Logan, a large noble-looking man, threw his blanket over his shoulder and spoke slowly and with power. "I appeal to any white man to say if ever he entered Logan's cabin hungry and I gave him not meat—if he ever came cold or naked and I gave him not clothing.

"At the beginning of this long and bloody war, Logan remained in his tent, an advocate of peace. Nay, such was my love for the whites that those of my own country pointed to me as they passed and said, 'Logan is the friend of the white man.' I had even thought to live with you, but for the crimes of Colonel Cresap. Last spring, in cold blood and unprovoked, he cut down all of my relatives, not sparing even women and children. There runs not a drop of my blood in the veins of any human being. This called upon me for revenge. I have sought it. I have killed many. I have fully glutted my vengeance. But now for my country I rejoice at the beams of peace. Yet do not harbor the thought that mine is the joy of fear. Logan never felt fear. He will not turn on his heel to save his life. Who is there to mourn for Logan? Not one."

Frontier Hero

As Simon listened sadly to these noble words, he felt that Logan had indeed been the friend of the whites and had been cruelly treated by them.

The treaty council finally decided that the Indians would make the Ohio River their eastern boundary, while the Virginians agreed not to pass beyond it to the west. With the formalities over, Lord Dunmore suggested a celebration and a campfire was built in the center of a vast clearing in the forest. Simon watched hundreds of warriors shout and shuffle and stamp in their tribal dances, while others chanted their weird songs to the pounding of drums.

After the useless peace treaty was signed, Simon was given his discharge at Fort Pitt, under his assumed name of Simon Butler. He took a room at Duncan's Tavern for a few days while he made plans for his future, knowing already what he desired most to do. For four years he had been obsessed by Yeager's tales of the marvels of Kaintuck-ee and wanted to go there. Hearing that Strader was dead he looking around for a companion, ruling out going with a group because many minds were likely to disagree.

Finally he found a sturdy, brown-eyed man, Thomas Williams, who had the same liking for exploring and adventure that Simon Kenton had. (He still used the name Butler.) Together they bought a canoe and stocked it with blankets, flour, salt, ammunition and traps. Simon knew that this trip downriver would be more dangerous now than the first two, for the Indians would be watching, ready to pick off anyone who got too close to the boundary line.

His partner proved to be a good hunter and woodsman,

In Search of Kain-Tuck-Ee

and they lived on the country as they floated downstream, pulling the canoe up on the bank in some hiding place every evening. But after two hundred miles of travel Williams started to scoff at the idea of there being any cane lands, and even Simon began to wonder if there were such a region.

Then they came to Letart's Falls where they found a French trader, and Simon told him that they were seeking the cane lands of Kain-tuck-ee. "Have you ever heard of such a place?" he asked.

The trader nodded. "Go to Limestone Creek," he said. "Turn into it and moor your canoe. Walk inland for a few miles and you will come to the place where the cane lands begin."

"How will we know Limestone Creek?" Simon asked.

The trader traced a crude map in the dirt and tried to describe the location of the stream.

The pair of explorers floated on for nearly two hundred miles more, but mistook Cabin Creek for Limestone Creek. Going up it a short distance, they then trudged inland for many weary miles without finding anything that looked like cane lands.

"There is no such place," Williams said in exasperation and fatigue.

Simon himself wondered just then if the place might be a dream of Yeager's. Yet he felt in his heart that there was such a region, and he determined to keep searching until he found it. They went down the river for two days, passing Limestone without knowing it, then pushed their way up another creek and explored inland without success.

Frontier Hero

"Cold weather is coming soon," Simon said wearily, "so we'd best leave exploring until another season and find a good location for camp."

Williams agreed readily and they went back up the Ohio to the mouth of the Big Sandy, near where Simon had camped before. Once settled, they put out traps and prepared for a winter of hunting.

The following spring they returned to Letart's Falls with a good winter's catch of furs to trade for supplies.

"We never found the cane lands," Simon told the trader.

"Then," the Frenchman said, "you missed Limestone Creek."

Again he traced the shore line, marking a place which he described as a natural landing port and the best on the river.

"We'll try again," Simon declared, "and take corn enough for parching and for planting. I feel in my bones that we are going to find the cane lands this time."

"I'm willing to give it another try," Williams agreed.

They studied the shore line carefully as they went along and this time found the landing place at Limestone Creek. Their camp was set up by late afternoon—too late, said Williams, to do any exploring. But Simon was too eager to wait until the next day, and he set out immediately, following the creek for a distance, then going westward.

Topping a rise he drew in his breath sharply, then blinked his eyes to make sure that what he saw was not a dream. His heart almost stopped beating. There in front of him it lay. The paradise for which he had been searching so long! Great dry stalks as big around as a small tree

In Search of Kain-Tuck-Ee

towered twice his height, while their tender green shoots were already as tall as he was. What a fertile land to grow such giant cane, and what a wonderous sight!

He stretched his arms up high and cried, "I've found it at last! It really exists, the land of my dreams. Kain-tuck-ee! This is mine, all mine, and I'm rich! I'll take up claims enough to make all of my family rich. I'll bring them here to live and found an empire!"

He walked among the canes, embracing them—laughing aloud with joy and exaltation. Finally the urge to tell Williams the good news surged over him and he began to retrace his steps. Suddenly a doe stepped in sight. Simon raised his rifle and fired. The animal dropped.

Again he laughed aloud in triumph. This was a good omen. Seizing the carcass he threw it across his strong shoulders and carried it back toward camp—a symbol of the good fortune of this memorable day.

It was nearly dark when he strode into the light of the campfire Williams had blazing and heaved his game down.

"I found it!" Simon cried at the top of his voice. "The canebrakes! They are real!" Then in a more reverent tone he added, "It's the most wonderful place in the world. It isn't a dream. We're rich!"

That night they celebrated the triumphant end of the long search by eating Simon's favorite food—the ham of a young deer.

"This," Simon said as he loosened his belt, "is the best eating I've ever enjoyed."

For several days the two explorers wandered about seeking the best new campsite, and at last selected a place where Simon had first discovered the canebrake. It was a beautiful spot with a clear spring on it. Here he and Williams cleared an acre of ground, after putting up a half-faced cabin, and planted corn. Thus they took "planting possession" of land in what would later be Mason County, Kentucky, and raised the first crop of corn ever cultivated by white men north of the Kentucky River.

CHAPTER 4

Indian Troubles Increase

Simon remembered vividly the Indian attack on his former camp, when he was without gun or knife or even his pants, and now prepared for such a surprise. Extra clothing was hidden in a hollow tree; knives and tomahawks were secreted in places where they might easily come to knowing hands but not be found by prowling savages. Rifles were always ready.

He and Williams established "tomahawk rights" to the land they claimed by girdling trees at the corners of their tract, and used the same weapons to cultivate their corn. While their crop ripened they explored the region around their plot of ground.

"Why should such rich land lack settlers?" Simon asked one day as they hunted.

"Don't know," Williams answered, puzzled. "It would be the finest sort of country for farms. But we are lucky to be the first ones here. We can take the pick of the land before anyone comes."

"I never liked farming," Simon admitted, "but a man

Frontier Hero

could get rich taking up and selling land. I intend to establish an empire in that way. Meantime, in such a hunters' paradise as this we can make a fortune in a winter of trapping for furs."

They explored Indian war roads marked by blazes and drawings of men, animals, suns and moons on trees. And they found buffalo trails on ridges and along creeks, tramped down to the bare rock. One day Simon counted 1500 buffaloes marching along one of these roads and followed them to a spring where salty water bubbled from the ground. Deer, elk and many smaller animals came to this salt lick from miles around.

Now and then he and Williams killed a young cow buffalo for food and for robes, but mainly they liked the meat of young deer or turkey. They lived well on a variety of game and fish, wild berries and fruit. Later when the corn ripened they had roasting ears and hominy, and between stones ground up some of the kernels into meal for corn pone.

All this while Simon's mind was acting like a sponge, soaking up facts about the country which he was systematically exploring. But he did not know that close to him, even overlapping the land he claimed, small settlements were springing up.

One day Kenton (known as Butler) and Williams went to gather salt at a place they had named Blue Licks, where they had set up a temporary camp. They were startled to see two white men coming up the trail, but so great was their pleasure at seeing people of their own race that tears came to their eyes.

Indian Troubles Increase

"I'm Hendricks, and this is Fitzpatrick," one of the men said. "As we were coming down the Ohio a squall hit us and our canoe overturned. We lost our guns, ammunition and all of our supplies. Sure thought we would starve to death or be killed by Indians."

"We have yet to see our first Indian around here," Simon assured them, "and we can fix you up with supplies at our main camp. My partner and I will help you build another canoe. Where are you headed?"

"We were on our way," Fitzpatrick explained, "to the other white settlements in Kentucky."

"Other settlements!" Simon exclaimed. "Williams and I don't know of any other settlements."

"But there are some," Fitzpatrick insisted. "The French trader at Letart's Falls told us of them. Also of yours."

Simon shrugged. "He should know. Settlers would naturally stop at his trading post."

Fitzpatrick said with a worried frown, "White settlements here are sure few and far between, and with so much game there must be Indians all around. Now that our canoe is wrecked and our supplies lost, I've had enough. Hendricks, I say we ought to go home."

"Not me. I'm staying," Hendricks announced firmly.

Finally it was arranged that Hendricks remain at the salt lick, while Simon and Williams took Fitzpatrick to their main camp, gave him supplies and a canoe and sent him on upriver.

Five days later Simon and Williams returned to their camp at Blue Licks, only to find the place completely wrecked and Hendricks gone.

Frontier Hero

Not far away they saw smoke rising from a ravine.

"The Injuns found us at last," Simon said. "Poor Hendricks! The red varmints must have him. He couldn't have escaped." He wondered what would become of him and Williams now. Would the savages put an end to his dream of founding an empire?

They hid in the forest all night and until late the next day when they crept silently to the ravine where they had seen the smoke. The Indians had gone, but their campfire still smouldered, and in it Simon and Williams found a human skull and bones.

Simon exclaimed in horror, "These could have been your bones or mine!"

"That's right," Williams said, warily glancing about, "and I'm for making tracks away from here. We've discovered a grand, fair land, but we'll never enjoy it dead."

"You mean give up our claim?" Simon asked.

Williams nodded. "The Injuns will show us no more mercy than they showed poor Hendricks."

Simon paused, thinking, then said determinedly, "I'm staying. We just won't camp so near the salt lick where the Injuns will come to hunt. This is big wilderness, with room enough for all. We've covered many miles around without seeing a redskin. They likely won't bother us. And we're far from the buffalo trail. . . ."

Williams listened and finally agreed to remain, mainly because he did not want to risk making the trip alone back to the Ohio. Settled in at their base camp once again, they saw no other human being in the area until one day when Simon was hunting near Blue Licks. He and Williams still

Indian Troubles Increase

hunted there but were always doubly alert when they did. A deer was approaching the salt lick and Simon slowly raised his rifle. Then hearing a light crackling sound behind him he whirled and saw an Indian with his gun aimed at the same animal.

Simon knew that if he did not get the Indian first, the Indian would get him, so he shot instantly. As the Indian fell, Simon waited with fast-beating heart, expecting other redskins to appear. When time went by and the forest remained silent, his heart finally resumed its normal beat and he went on hunting until he got a deer.

On another occasion, while climbing up a game trail he bumped right into an Indian at the top. Both drew back startled, but Simon recovered instantly.

"How!" Simon said, judging that a show of friendliness was the best policy.

"How!" grunted the Indian in surprise.

Simon held out his hand and they shook hands in the white man's way.

Then the Indian pointed at Simon's powder horn which was almost empty, and at first Simon thought the redskin meant that he was poorly equipped for fighting. But the Indian surprised him by pouring half of his own powder into Simon's horn saying, "More hunt."

"Thank you," Simon said amazed. "Thank you."

The native nodded and went on down the trail Simon had just come up, while Simon continued in the direction from which the Indian had popped over the hill.

In the fall Simon was again on a hunt near the Blue Licks, when he was forced to climb a tree to escape being

Frontier Hero

trampled by a herd of buffaloes pounding along the trail. Looking around he was dumbfounded to see someone in a nearby tree.

"Show yourself," Simon ordered.

"Show yourself first," the person shouted.

"Ho!" Simon called. "You're a white man."

"Of course. So you're a white man, too! What are you doing on this trail?"

"I have a camp near here," Simon replied. "Come have supper with me."

"Obliged. Just as soon as these beasts clear the trail."

Later, the man introduced himself as John Hinkston and said that he had put up several cabins about forty miles away. Simon and Williams promised to visit his station when they could.

Within a month Simon came onto another white man at Blue Licks, Michael Stoner. He told about several other settlements in Kentucky, one in particular named Boonesborough after its founder, Daniel Boone. Stoner praised Boone as a man respected by everyone—a good hunter, a fine woodsman and one with the gift of leadership. Simon decided that he would have to meet this person.

Late in the fall Simon and Williams set out to visit the other settlements and to get acquainted with their frontier brothers.

Simon had a clear description of the location of these settlements from Stoner, and this, coupled with his uncanny knack of finding his way through wilderness, enabled him to find them without difficulty. He and Williams spent the entire winter going from one station to

Indian Troubles Increase

another, visiting the settlers, and Simon acted as hunter to pay for his keep wherever he went. He first stopped at Hinkston's blockhouse, then went on to Riddle's Station. Next, he stayed at McClelland's Station (where Georgetown is now), then Harrodsburg, and finally Boonesborough, where he met Daniel Boone.

Boone was a tall, bronzed, dark-haired man, and in his gray eyes was the look of one used to leadership. Simon felt an instant bond of friendship. Here, he felt, was a worthwhile person of strong character with whom he would like to be friends.

Simon and Williams returned later to Hinkston's blockhouse, where Simon became hunter for the settlers, and there he bought two dogs, Nip and Tuck, to help in his job.

In the middle of the winter when ice and snow held the land in their grip, Simon took his two dogs and went out for game. Suddenly a lone buffalo bull appeared on the trail. Instantly the dogs rushed the beast and jumped up and seized him by the ears. The three animals went tumbling down the icy hill together and slid out upon the frozen river. The tremendous weight of the buffalo broke the ice and all the animals plunged into the water.

Simon gasped, hoping that his dogs would rise to the surface, but though he waited a long time they did not do so. He returned from his hunt empty-handed, deeply depressed by the accident that had taken the two animals that had become his friends and helpers.

Offered other dogs to take their place he refused, saying, "No other animals can replace kinfolk like Nip and Tuck. They were just like members of my family."

Frontier Hero

In the spring of 1776 Simon and Williams returned to their camp on the Lawrence. Soon Samuel Arrowsmith joined them and started to clear an acre of land adjoining their cornfield. Simon left most of his planting to Williams, for he found himself now with a new job that took up most of his time.

Settler parties were coming down the river in waves and most of them turned in at the natural landing at Limestone Creek. It was a joy for them to find a competent young woodsman who walked like an Indian and could find his way through the wilderness like a native. Simon was able to guide these explorers to all of the settlements, where everyone was his friend. Several new places were started and those already in existence gained new members. It seemed that the fame of Kentucky's fair and fertile land had spread throughout the East, and people were pouring in.

After the Dunmore War the Indians for a time had been friendly. But in 1776 the Indians rose up, raiding, stealing, killing and driving off horses and cattle. The new pioneers brought word of the American Revolution, then a year old, and the dreadful news that the Indians were being urged on by the British. English gold, and seeing more and more colonial settlers claim their land, was firing up the tribes to make war.

In June 1776, word came by messenger that all of the explorers and settlers of Kentucky were to meet at Harrodsburg to elect someone to go to Virginia to ask for aid. George Rogers Clark and John Gabriel Jones were selected to go. At the meeting Simon was happy to renew

Indian Troubles Increase

his friendship with Clark, whom he had learned to admire during their previous association.

Returned to his farm, where he and Williams had planted two acres of corn, Simon found that buffaloes had trampled their field and left little for the squirrels and raccoons to finish. Discouraged by this and alarmed by the increasing Indian depredations they decided to go to Hinkston's blockhouse or one of the other stations.

Arrowsmith decided to go with them, but before leaving he buried the large kettle he had brought for boiling salt, and several other large pieces of equipment.

Simon turned his back on his camp sadly, yet determined to return to it one day when the Indian troubles were over.

They found all of the settlements they came to abandoned, until they arrived at McClelland's Station, where George Rogers Clark arrived soon with his companion, John Gabriel Jones.

He said to Simon, "We were bringing in five hundred pounds of powder and a quantity of lead when we were jumped by Indians, so we hid the ammunition on the lower of Three Islands and escaped."

"Tell me where you hid it and I'll take a group of men and bring it in," Simon said. "We need it."

Clark asked for volunteers for this dangerous mission, selecting thirty men to be led by Simon to Three Islands. The trip was successful. But when they returned with the ammunition they found all of the settlers at McClelland's Station in deepest gloom.

There had been so many reports of murderous Indian

raids that everyone had decided to retreat to Harrodsburg and this move touched Simon deeply. Children wailed; women wept; men were morose and tense. Now of all the settlements, only Boonesborough and Harrodsburg remained.

Soon there came from Virginia, which had jurisdiction over Kentucky, a commission that gave George Rogers Clark the title of major. It put him in command of the frontier, with power to appoint his own officers. Daniel Boone, Harrod and Logan were then raised to the rank of captain.

The settlers spent a miserable winter at Harrodsburg but were not attacked. However, they frequently saw Indians lurking about, so there was a constant sense of danger and uncertainty about the place.

By spring the settlers were in desperate need of clothes. Simon, John Haggin and four others were sent to Hinkston's Station to bring back the flax and hemp that had been abandoned there at the time of the retreat. These materials combined with buffalo hair would make sturdy cloth.

Haggin, riding out ahead of the rest, sighted a band of Indians and galloped back to report.

Simon said, "We had better go back to the fort."

"What are you? A coward?" Haggin sneered. "No brave man would think of turning back without giving the Injuns a battle."

Kenton felt his face flush. "This isn't a time to argue," he snapped. "I'll go as far and fire as fast as any man."

Indian Troubles Increase

"Then let's give the redskins a teach," shouted Haggin, his eyes flashing.

The men dismounted and tied their horses to nearby trees, but no sooner were they afoot than they were attacked on all sides. It would have meant certain death or capture to stand and fight the hordes around them, and at a shout from Simon each man took off for himself. By some miracle they all managed to get back to the fort alive, but lost all of their horses.

Simon later thought wryly how careless he had been to allow Haggin to goad him into making a foolish move against the enemy. He had learned a lesson.

Simon and his party were able to make the journey to Hinkston's Station shortly after, and returned safely with the materials for clothes which were so badly needed. Then Harrodsburg was attacked by the Shawnee led by Chief Black Fish. It was fortunate that Simon and his men were there, for with their added guns the attack was finally beaten off.

Nearly all of the settlers who were able to had gone back to Virginia, leaving only about one hundred and fifty men to defend the raging frontier. These men, like Simon, were so constantly occupied with just staying alive from day to day that they paid little attention to the American Revolution then being fought in the East.

In the winter of 1777 Boone appointed Kenton (still known as Butler) as hunter for the hungry settlers. He risked his life every moment of this work, and it made his days of acting as a scout seem easy in comparison.

Frontier Hero

Although he was known as one of the bravest of frontiersmen, on many a lonely night in the forest he knew fear.

His method was to creep from the fort at night and get to the place where he was to hunt the next day. The nights were cold and it was dangerous to build a fire. But he had long ago discovered that white oak bark would burn without smoke. He would dig a hole in the ground about the size of his head, place layers of the bark within it and set it afire with flint and steel. Using his blanket as a shield served to hide the small blaze from prowling savages. When the bark was burning he covered it with dirt, leaving two air holes for draft. Then sitting propped against a tree, feet toward the fire and rifle in hand, he went to sleep.

In the morning he set out to hunt. When he found his game and fired a shot he drew back at once and hid in the bushes. Then for a long while he waited, watching and listening to see if the sound had attracted the enemy.

If no one appeared he dragged the kill to the nearest tree and stood with his back against it for protection while he skinned his animal. Spreading the hide on the ground, he cut up the meat and placed the portions he wanted on the skin, making a pouch of it. When he had killed and butchered another animal, he heaved the two bundles upon his shoulders and carried them to camp.

Simon kept the settlers alive that winter with the meat he provided. Without salt or bread, it was all they had to eat, weeks at a time.

During those lonely, cold nights while he sat propped against a tree he often thought of his family. Would he ever see them again? Had he been able to remain at home

Indian Troubles Increase

he would now be a tenant farmer like his father and his brother William, and toil from dawn to dark at unprofitable work. But it would be a secure life. There were no Indians on the warpath near Bull Run Mountain. Now, however, Simon was in constant danger of losing his life. As for profit, would he ever be able to return to his claim? Would he even live to realize his dream of founding an empire?

CHAPTER 5

Troubled Times

One day Simon was summoned to the cabin of George Rogers Clark. "As you know," Clark said, "I have the responsibility of commanding the western frontier. I need scouts, but unfortunately there is no money with which to pay them. Will you serve with no recompense but the gratitude of Virginia?"

"I will," Simon replied.

Clark nodded, obviously pleased. "I knew I could count on you. I assign you to act as chief of scouts for Harrodsburg. Pick out half a dozen men to work with you. This, of course, will be in addition to your duty as hunter for this fort. You have kept us from starving to death in the past; we can't dispense with your service in that respect."

Simon said gravely, "I can combine the two duties if I hunt during the daytime."

"That," Major Clark frowned, "will be more dangerous than the method you've been using."

"I know, sir. But I can watch out for Indian signs by daylight."

Troubled Times

Game remained plentiful and Simon did not have to go so far away to hunt. As a scout, twice within the month of February that sixth sense he had developed told him that Indians were near and he warned the settlers in time to drive the savages off. March and April brought severe storms which hampered the work of fortifying the place, but they also prevented attacks by Black Fish and his warriors. At all times, however, some Indians remained close by to snipe at everyone who went out to get needed firewood. Later in the spring, when the settlers had to go out to the field to plant corn for the following winter, they worked with guards posted over them. Meanwhile, Simon fulfilled his double duty.

Word then came from Boonesborough that the families there were without meat, and Clark sent him to hunt for them for a few days. Simon was glad for this opportunity to renew his friendship with the man he admired, Daniel Boone.

His visit was interrupted by a sudden attack by Black Fish and over a hundred of his warriors. Without warning, Indians sprang out from every side of the forest and fired upon the workers who were planting corn. They fled back toward the fort, but about fifty yards from the gate an Indian overtook the rear man, felled him with his tomahawk and began to scalp his victim. Simon ran out and shot the scalper, and with two other men began to chase the attackers.

Boone came out with ten men to help, leaving only eight men inside to protect the women and children within the fort. Seeing this the band of Indians instantly rushed in

Frontier Hero

between the little party of whites and the fort, cutting them off. At that moment Simon saw an Indian aim at Boone and with his deadly quickness shot the savage.

"Return to the fort," Boone shouted.

This meant that the men should fire, then without taking time to reload, use their rifle butts and club their way through the Indian line. Simon, however, calmly took time to reload. Long practice had made him unusually quick with this operation upon which his life had depended many times. It took great skill to reload the clumsy old rifles on the run, but he accomplished this difficult task twice on his way back to the fort.

During this brief battle seven were wounded, among them Boone, who had his leg broken by a shot. Simon saw an Indian standing over the captain, tomahawk upraised for the kill. Instantly he fired and brought the red man down, then stooped and raised Boone across his shoulders. Dodging and shifting he finally carried him through the entrance. The other settlers who had not been shot down came racing in and managed to swing the gate shut in the faces of the howling savages.

Simon took Boone to his cabin and laid him upon his bed of cornhusks.

"Simon," Boone said, "I was lucky to have you with me today. You are the bravest man I know."

"I only did what any man would do," Simon said.

For another month those within the fort lived in a state of constant siege. Their cattle were killed, their horses were stolen, and they dared not venture from the fortress to work their crops, for the Shawnee perched in trees wait-

Troubled Times

ing to shoot down anyone who ventured outside the gate. Nevertheless the people within the stockade had to eat, so Simon continued his dangerous hunting and always brought in the desperately needed meat.

Attacks and counterattacks against the Indians went on all along the frontier through the winter of 1778. Captain Watkins with three men, a woefully small party, was finally sent from Virginia to aid, but the men of the East were busy fighting the British and more could not be spared.

Meantime, Major George Rogers Clark had gone to Virginia to enlist aid against the British, who were inciting the Indians, but succeeded in getting only a few volunteers. With them he descended the Ohio and camped on an island near the falls. From there he sent messengers to Boone's and Harrod's stations asking for men to join him in an expedition against the British settlements on the Mississippi. Those at the forts considered that the few men they had should stay to defend them. Simon and Haggin, being unmarried, were the only ones to join Clark's company.

Clark was disgusted to receive such a poor showing from the settlements; he considered that the cause of the whole country was more important than defending the frontier. He was firm in his opinion that if the British could be defeated, the Indian troubles would solve themselves. However, he did enlist a dozen men who had been making salt at Drennan's Lick, and with them Clark's force amounted to 153.

Simon realized that this was a woefully small party for so hazardous an expedition. They went downriver to

Frontier Hero

Cherokee Fort, now abandoned, and sank their canoes there. Then taking their supplies and equipment upon their backs, they slogged their way through the wilderness, guided by Simon, one hundred miles to Kaskaskia. The town and fort were commanded by one called merely "the governor."

Clark told Simon that if they could take the fort, the town would have to surrender. "We will attack at midnight," Major Clark said. "Scout around and try to find a weak point."

Simon set out, his moccasined feet making no sound, and soon came upon a little cabin outside the fort with a light in it. He sent word back, and when Clark came up he ordered the cabin surrounded. They found a Frenchman living there who hastily admitted that he had little love for the British.

"They have no sentinels posted," he told them readily. "And I know a spot where the pickets of their stockade are so rotten you can easily break them and enter."

"Show us," Clark ordered.

The Frenchman pointed out the weak place, and the entire party of Americans entered without being discovered. Then their willing guide showed them where the governor slept.

Simon and Clark entered and wakened him. As the Britisher sat up in bed, Simon had to grin. The man looked so ridiculous with a red stocking cap all askew and a mixed expression of surprise and utter dismay on his face.

"I—I—surrender," he stammered.

Troubled Times

"What about your comrades?" Clark asked in a sharp voice.

"I—I—surrender them all," the governor added.

This victory, accomplished without firing a shot, was of great advantage to the frontier, because the fort remained in possession of the Colonials throughout the war.

A few days later Clark sent Simon with three others to carry messages to Colonel Bowman, who was then in command at Harrodsburg.

"Go by way of Vincennes," Clark ordered. "Scout the place and see if it can be taken. But if there is danger of your being captured, commit your papers to memory and destroy them. Under no condition allow them to be taken by the enemy."

"They'll not get them," Simon promised.

Nearing Vincennes, he and his comrades hid by day and scouted by night. He had memorized the contents of the papers he carried and had destroyed them. After he had scouted the strength and condition of Vincennes he sent a man back to Clark with the information and continued with the other men to Harrodsburg, which they reached on the thirteenth day.

At the fort, Daniel Boone called Simon and proposed that he join an expedition against an Indian village on Paint Creek. (Simon was still using the name of Butler in place of his rightful one, Kenton.)

"You're as much good to me as five ordinary men," Boone told him.

Simon was weary, but he promptly agreed to join Boone's force of twenty men. When they were still some miles from the village they were met by a party of more than fifty Indians. But Boone's little force of seasoned fighters attacked with vigor and drove off the warriors.

Calling his men together Boone said, "The Indians now know of our approach. We can't surprise them. To make an open attack on their village with our small force is too dangerous. We will return to the fort."

"I'd like to stay around and scout their village," Simon said.

"I'll go with you," Alexander Montgomery volunteered.

The two scouts were able to capture several horses and started back for the fort, but on the way they discovered an Indian trail leading toward Boonesborough. They turned off then toward Logan's Station, and arriving there learned that the Indians whose trail they had crossed had attacked Boonesborough. The whites had lost two men but the redskins had suffered heavily and given up the siege. Simon and Montgomery rode on to the fort.

Simon continued to serve as hunter until the first of September. During this time there had not been any Indian attacks, but the natives stole their horses until there were not enough left to work the fields. George Rogers Clark, Alexander Montgomery and Simon decided to go out among the Indian villages and recover some of their stolen animals.

They crossed the Ohio and pushed on to the Indian village, Chillicothe, carrying salt to entice the horses and halters with which to lead them. They hid out during the day, but by night discovered a herd of horses feeding on the prairie. The men managed to capture and get halters

Troubled Times

on seven of the animals, then rode swiftly through the night to the Ohio. With the dawn came winds of almost hurricane force, and the horses refused to enter the turbulent water. Finally Simon and his companions were forced to give up their attempts to get the beasts to cross the river. They rode back into the hills, where they hobbled the horses and turned them out to graze.

The next day they went down again to the Ohio with the captured stock. The wind and waves had calmed but the horses still refused to enter the water. Simon and the other two men were sorely disappointed; the need of the settlers for these animals was great. Because of Indian danger in that area they hastily decided to turn four of the horses loose. They would ride the other three to the falls of the Ohio where some of Major Clark's men were stationed.

After they had gone a short distance, they reconsidered. They had been foolish to let the spare horses go, and made up their minds to try to round them up again. The men spread out then to round up the freed animals.

Simon had not ridden far when he heard war whoops from the direction where they had tried to ford the river. Dismounting, he quickly tied his horse behind a clump of brush and stole cautiously up a high bank overlooking the Ohio.

CHAPTER 6

Captured!

No sooner had Simon reached the top of the embankment than he ran head-on into a small war party. It was impossible for him to retreat so he aimed his rifle at the foremost Indian, hoping to frighten off the band by making them think that he was a member of a large party of whites. Then his gun flashed in the pan. He turned and ran through the brush with the howling savages in pursuit, racing through an area where a hurricane had torn up great trees. The trunks offered him some protection, for the Indians on horseback could not follow him here. But by the noise they made, Simon knew that the Indians had separated and were pursuing him on either side of the fallen timber.

As he reached the bottom of the hill where the windfall ended, one of the Indians rode up boldly, jumped off his horse and rushed at him with upraised tomahawk. There had been no time to reload, so Simon grabbed his gun by the barrel and started to swing it as a club when he was grabbed from behind.

Captured!

In a moment he was surrounded by howling savages, and while they were binding his arms, Alexander Montgomery galloped up. He shot at the Indians, missed and fled with several redskins in pursuit. They fired and Montgomery fell. Then the Indians leaped upon him with screeches of triumph and soon returned to wave Montgomery's scalp before Simon's horrified eyes. He hoped fervently that Clark had escaped, and since no one returned with his scalp, Simon judged that he had done so.

The Indians camped that night on the bank of the Ohio and held a victory dance over the hapless Montgomery's scalp. Simon was forced to watch. Tomorrow, he thought, his own scalp would be the savages' cause for celebration. He was seated with his back against a tree and securely tied there during the night. Unable to sleep, the dark hours dragged as he thought of the fate that was in store for him. He determined to try to escape, but with no hope that he would succeed. He wanted to bring a speedy end to his life by arrow or gun, rather than the slow agonies of death by torture.

In the morning Simon watched his captors eating their breakfast, but they did not offer him any. They would not waste food upon one who was so soon to die. And before he died, he learned from their conversation, he would furnish them with grim amusement.

Jabbering and laughing as they looked over the horses, the Indians selected a huge stallion, which was obviously the wildest animal in the herd. After they had caught him it took four of them to hold him. Then they lifted Simon to the stallion's back, face up, tied his legs together under its belly and his arm under the horse's neck. Another rope was looped under the stallion's tail in order to make him buck.

When Simon had been so securely tied that he could not fall off, the Indians whipped the stallion and sent him bucking and plunging through the thick underbrush. They whooped with laughter when they saw Simon being scratched and torn by briars and branches during the wild ride.

"Do you want to steal any more horses?" they yelled as the horse lunged, reared and kicked viciously to dislodge his unwelcome burden.

"What a way to die!" Simon thought, clenching his teeth hard to keep from crying out in agony. He knew his torturers would relish any sign of weakness.

The savages soon tired of the game when no sound of pain came from Simon, and the stallion, worn out and wet with sweat from exertion, calmly rejoined the herd. Now the Indians rode toward Chillicothe, the exhausted stallion following and making no further attempts to throw Simon.

Bleeding from his many cuts and scratches, badly bruised, thirsty and hungry, he was left tied in his uncomfortable position until the Indians made camp. Then Simon was lifted from the horse and given a piece of meat and some water. Later his shirt was jerked from him and he was thrown on the ground with his arms and legs outstretched and tied to stakes. A rope tied around his neck and fastened to a tree was just tight enough to choke him if he made any motion.

Before they went to their sleeping robes the Indians

Captured!

danced around him, kicking and beating him. Finally they left him lying the whole night in his painful bonds, the prey of gnats and mosquitoes.

The next day he was tied upon the stallion's back in the same manner as before; but the animal was broken now and did not buck or dash wildly through the woods. He followed the herd quite meekly, and Simon was grateful for this one small bit of good fortune.

That night he was again spread-eagled on the ground, and for three nights more after they reached camp outside the village. Then the natives there all came out to whoop and yell as they danced about Simon, kicking him and beating him with sticks.

He gritted his teeth and made no outcry that would satisfy his captors, while hours seemed to go by as the Indians amused themselves by torturing him. Finally, however, they grew weary and returned to the village.

Simon was so exhausted that despite the torments of the gnats and mosquitoes and his numerous wounds, he slept fitfully.

Early the next morning the natives again came from their village to have more fun with their prisoner. They formed two lines about six feet apart, each savage armed with a stout club, and Simon realized that he must run the gantlet.

He was a swift runner and the Indians had scarcely hit him as he drew near the end of the line; but there he saw one with a knife ready to slash him. Knowing that this was against their savage rules of the game Simon broke through the line and raced toward the village. The council

Frontier Hero

house would be in the center of it, and he knew that if he made this haven without being caught he would not have to run the gantlet again.

Hundreds of yelling savages were after him in full pursuit, and just as he reached the edge of the village he was met by a warrior on guard. This man was fresh; Simon was on the point of exhaustion. The Indian leaped upon him, throwing him to the ground, and instantly he was set upon by his angry pursuers. They avenged themselves on him for running away by kicking, beating and clubbing him over the head.

He endured the punishment without dying or even fainting, and presently the Indians wearied of their savage sport. They allowed Simon to sit up and gave him a drink of water, but not out of mercy. They did not want him to die too quickly.

As soon as he recovered sufficiently to walk he was taken to the council house, where the warriors would decide what his fate should be. The men sat in a circle with an old chief in the center, and several of the natives rose to make impassioned speeches. Although Simon knew some of the language, they spoke so fast that he could not understand all they said. But he caught enough to know they were speaking for or against his death. Those who advocated mercy were received with frowns; those who urged his death were greeted with shouts of approval.

When the arguing was over, the man near the entrance picked up a war club and started passing it around the circle. Shortly Simon realized that this was their method of voting. Those who wanted him to die struck the club

Captured!

heavily upon the ground; those who favored allowing him to live merely passed the club to the next man. Meanwhile the old chief recorded the votes on two sides of a stick with his knife. It did not take Simon long to see that most of the warriors favored his death, and his heart seemed to shrivel within him.

He looked toward the entrance, thinking that a dash for freedom would gain him a quick death, for he knew their method of execution was usually by burning at the stake. But the Indian next to him seemed to sense what was in Simon's mind, for he grunted and put out a strong hand to hold him.

When the war club had been passed around the circle the Indians gave wild shouts of joy: their prisoner must die. And he would provide them with the supreme amusement by burning at the stake.

The question now argued was about the time and place of his burning. Some wished the event to take place immediately; others wanted to take him on to Wapatomika, where more people could witness the occasion. The next morning he was put on a horse and driven toward the place of execution. On the way they passed two other villages, and he was forced to run the gantlet in both. Weak now and unable to run with his usual speed, he was badly beaten each time.

Knowing he was exhausted the Shawnee thought that he lacked the strength to try to escape, so he was carelessly watched. Noting this, Simon worked his hands free from their thongs and stood with them still behind him. He rested his head on his chest, his eyes seemingly closed as

Frontier Hero

though he were dozing, but his mind was wide awake scheming.

He was on the edge of the village and guarded by a sleepy brave. Watching carefully, when the guard's eyes finally closed, Simon was ready. He tiptoed off into the nearby forest and then broke into a run. Soon he heard a wild yelling. His escape had been discovered, and the savages were after him. Fear lent wings to his feet; he was outdistancing his pursuers.

Finally the din behind him subsided. The Indians must have scattered through the woods to search silently for him. Then on the point of dropping from exhaustion, he slowed his pace and drew in the precious air in deep gasps.

Just as he thought he was safe a number of mounted Indians loomed before him, and with yowls of triumph drove him back to the village. Now he gave up hope. Death stared him in the face. He would not be given another opportunity of escaping. "Cutta-ho-tha" the condemned one, the Shawnee called him.

In the village he was given over to the young warriors to punish with torture. His hands were tied behind his back and he was rolled in the stream, then in the mud, time and again until he was nearly drowned by water and suffocated by mud.

Finally the Indians put him on a horse and took him to Wapatomika, where he was daubed with black paint to show that he was doomed to death. At this fairly large village the people crowded around to stare or shout insults at their victim or strike him with sticks.

Simon made hideous faces and hurled back worse insults

Captured!

at his enemies, hoping to goad one of them into killing him quickly. But they were too shrewd to be deprived of their sport. At last his head sank on his chest as hopelessness flooded over him.

Then he was taken roughly and tied against a dead tree trunk, while dried leaves and twigs were piled around his feet, with bigger pieces of wood on top. When the pile reached as high as his chest a lighted brand was thrust among the smaller branches.

Though his heart beat with terror, strangely enough Simon's glance darted around at the lovely landscape. What a beautiful world it was, although the sky was cloudy. Here was some of that wonderful, fertile land he had hoped to own someday. Now he would own nothing. He was going to die a horrible death by fire and be nothing before he had scarcely commenced to live.

The fire crackled and caught. The smoke blinded and choked him. Yet he kept silent before the savages. But inwardly he was saying, "I don't want to die! I am too young to die! Life is good...."

Now the orange flames were licking at the larger pieces of wood. With shouts of joy the Indians threw more fuel upon the heap.

"Pile the fire high," Simon shouted defiantly. "The sooner it is over the better."

Now he felt the heat and sweat burst from his pores. Soon the greedy flames would be eating at his flesh.

Then he felt a cool drop on his face, followed by another and another. The light of day had suddenly faded, and at first Simon thought the smoke had blotted it out. But suddenly he was being deluged by rain, and he remembered the cloudy sky. The water sizzled as it hit the flames, and soon the fire died down to a mere smoldering. Then it went out completely.

The Indians muttered in awe over this strange miracle which had quenched the flames that were to devour their victim. Simon could see by the expression on their faces that they considered the downpour a supernatural happening.

And Simon himself considered it so. Lifting his face heavenward he murmured, "Thank you, Father, for saving my life. I'll try to make it worthwhile."

The savages faded away to seek shelter from the storm in their lodges, leaving Simon tied to the tree. The rain was cold, but never had he felt anything so welcome as that heavy storm. But his relief was only temporary.

When the downpour finally ceased the Indians came and again painted Simon black, for the rain had washed him clean and white. Then they began looking around for fuel that was not too sodden to burn. They went about the task rather sullenly, as though they resented having had their fun spoiled earlier.

Simon's hopes sank. He had thought that the Indians would consider the rainstorm as an intervention by the Great Spirit, but evidently they had decided otherwise and were determined that he must die.

Seeing several men enter the camp Simon glumly concluded they were just visitors come to witness his death agonies. Then his head snapped up as he thought he heard a voice that he recognized. Peering into the crowd he saw

Captured!

a white man dressed in Indian garb. His black hair was long. He could pass for a native. But his tanned skin did not have the coppery tinge of the red man.

"Girty!" Simon cried out in sudden relief. "Girty! Don't you know me?"

Simon Girty stared at Simon Kenton but shook his head. Obviously he did not recognize his friend of the Dunmore War, painted black as he was.

"I'm Simon Butler," the prisoner cried, using his assumed name. "Don't you remember me? We were scouts together under Dunmore."

"Butler!" Girty shouted joyfully. "I did not know you under that black paint." He threw his arms around Simon, tears in his eyes.

"They sure plan to burn you," Girty whispered, holding him closely. "But I'll try to save you. I live with them and they have adopted me into their tribe. Maybe they will listen to me."

Girty immediately called a council, and as Simon was untied the warriors formed a circle around them. In the Indian language Girty made an impassioned plea in his friend's behalf. Simon was able to follow most of the speech and could see the fierceness fading from his captors' faces. Finally the Indians shouted and Kenton judged from their tone that they were voting to show him mercy. He was put in Girty's care.

"What can I do to show my gratitude?" Simon asked.

"Just be my friend," Girty answered gruffly. "I am loathed by most white men, and detest many of them in turn. But you are like my brother. You never thought meanly of me."

Kenton choked up. "You *are* my brother, for I owe you my life. I have always admired your courage, on the trail and as a scout. I'll never forget you."

Girty took Simon to the stream and helped him wash the paint from his body, carefully bathing the wounds in his head where he had been struck by a tomahawk. "You'll always have dents in your skull," he said.

Then Girty went on, "The British have a trading post not far from here. I will take you there and outfit you with clothes."

When this was done Girty also purchased a horse and saddle for his friend. Simon had no especial reason to return to civilization. He was a fugitive from justice and had always feared that he would run into someone who would know of his crime. Now that the savages were friendly to him he enjoyed riding with Girty from one Indian village to another as an honored guest in the lodges of the chiefs.

Simon would soon regret, however, that he had not gone as far from these savages as possible, for Girty received a message that he must bring him back to Wapatomika. Since a large party of redskins came bringing the message there was no choice but to return with them; and when they reached the council house the chief warriors were waiting. The Indians all arose and shook hands with Girty, but scowled at Simon and refused to shake his hand. Simon's heart fell. He could feel the hatred flow from the natives.

One of them stood and started to jabber and Girty

Captured!

turned to Simon. "They have just suffered a defeat from a detachment of whites," he related. "Several Indians were killed and others wounded. They are in the mood for revenge. They still want to burn you at the stake!"

Kenton felt a wave of weakness sweep over him. Why hadn't he escaped when he had the chance! He had even considered living among these Indians as Girty did. It had seemed a most pleasant life, riding from village to village, living on the land.

Girty rose and again delivered an impressive speech, but this time the anger and hatred did not fade from the Indians' faces. What little hope he yet had faded from Simon as his glance swept the circle of dark, scowling faces.

After Girty finished speaking the vote was taken, and this time it was overwhelmingly in favor of death.

"I can do nothing more," Girty said hopelessly. "They are in a killing mood."

Nevertheless he again rose and spoke, this time more slowly. Simon gathered that he was suggesting that it was the time for them to go to the upper Sandusky to get their annuities from the British. They would not want to be late for this important event. And there they would meet many friends from other tribes. It would be far better to hold the burning of their prisoner until they arrived there, so that more people could enjoy the event.

A shout of approval met this suggestion.

"The more delay, the better your chance of escape," Girty muttered as he sat down beside Simon.

The next morning Girty set out with Simon, who was

accompanied by five young warriors as guard. The entire village came along to get their British pay, and Simon saw that he would be given no chance to escape his terrible fate.

On their way to upper Sandusky they passed through the village of Scioto where the famed Chief Logan lived. Simon and his guards stayed in the lodge of the chief overnight, and Logan talked with him.

"I will ask that you stay here tomorrow," Logan said. "Meanwhile I will send messengers on to upper Sandusky to plea for your life. I can make no promises, but will do all I can. Although your whites massacred every member of my family and the blood of Logan flows in no one's veins, Logan is the friend of every man. I will try to save you."

The messengers returned but Simon did not hear what news they brought. The next morning the guards set out to upper Sandusky with him, and though Logan shook hands in a friendly manner, he did not say whether his messengers had any success.

As they approached the meeting place all of the natives came out to meet the guard and stare at the prisoner. Simon expected to be made to run the gantlet again, but surprisingly enough this ordeal was not required of him. However, another grand council was held to determine his fate.

This time a French-Canadian, garbed in the gaudy attire of an English captain, stepped into the middle of the circle and commenced to talk with an air of authority.

"That is Pierre Druillard," Girty told Simon in a low voice. "He represents the British Indian Agency department and is a power around here. The Indians will prob-

Captured!

ably do as he says, because he decides whether to pay or withhold annuities. Logan probably sent his messengers to Druillard and your fate is in his hands."

"As you know," Druillard said, "the Americans are at war with our country. They call it a revolution. It is also well known that it is to the interest of the British that not an American should be left alive."

Simon's heart sank. This did not sound like a speech advocating mercy.

Druillard went on, "The Americans are the cause of the present bloody war. Neither peace nor safety can be expected as long as these intruders are permitted to live."

The Indians roared their approval.

Druillard bowed and continued. "That the war shall be carried on successfully requires shrewdness, as well as bravery. The information that we might gain from this prisoner might be of great advantage to us in conducting the future operation of the war. It could well be more valuable than his death would be. I am sure that the commanding officer at Detroit could wring information from him that will be of great value. I hope that in this case you will delay the death of the prisoner until I can take him to Detroit. After that he can be brought back and you can do as you please with the scoundrel...."

Hope rose anew in Simon. Anything might happen on the way to or in Detroit.

Druillard was not through speaking. "I know," he went on, "that you have suffered great troubles because of the prisoner. However, you recovered all of the horses he and his companions stole. You killed one of them, therefore

Frontier Hero

you have had some revenge. As further payments for your troubles I will give you one hundred dollars' worth of rum and tobacco, if you will allow me to take him to my commanding officer in Detroit."

The Indians shouted their approval of this proposal and Druillard paid the ransom. He then took Simon with two Indians to Detroit. There the French gave the two Indians further rewards and Simon was put in the guardhouse.

Simon was treated well. A wooden tub filled with warm water was provided, and he experienced the luxury of a bath. He tried to wash and comb his long hair, but it was so matted with blood, mud and burrs that a comb would not go through it and the prison guard shaved his head.

Relaxed on a cot, Simon thought about the events of the past weeks. Now it seemed like a dreadful dream. Although he was still a prisoner, the worst that could happen to him would be death before a firing squad. No longer need he fear being burned alive . . . unless Druillard kept his promise to the Indians and sent him back.

Hamilton, commander of the British army at Detroit, had gone to Vincennes. So Simon was questioned by Captain Lernoult, the commandant in charge, who tried to extract from him some idea of the strength of the Colonials in Kentucky. Simon was evasive, saying he had no idea of the number of soldiers, but he glibly named all of the officers he could think of who had ever been in Kentucky. Lernoult would then draw his own conclusion that with so many officers the fighting strength of the Americans must be considerable.

After the first day he was not imprisoned and was even

Captured!

allowed to roam the town. He was given two new buckskin suits, and permitted to draw rations from the stock of food.

The Indians who had come as guards with him to Detroit waited around in the hope of taking Simon back to their people to be burned. But after the British had told them repeatedly that he would not be given up they finally departed.

Simon was allowed to come and go as he pleased, so long as he answered for roll call each Sunday and made no attempt to cross the Ecorse River. Altogether, it was not an unpleasant captivity; he was even paid for doing odd jobs around the place. He wanted to buy a rifle, but he knew that a prisoner who owned a gun would be suspected of wanting to escape. However, he let it be known that he was an expert hunter and soon was allowed to go with hunting parties along the river for pigeons, ducks and geese. So the people got used to seeing him around the town carrying a borrowed rifle.

Simon had the gift of making friends wherever he was, and he made friends in Detroit, Lernoult among them. Many councils were held and Simon asked the captain if he might attend them, since time hung heavy on his hands. The commandant consented, so Simon sat in on them and while pretending to doze kept his ears wide open for information. At one of the councils a group of Indians came in from an expedition to Pennsylvania, bringing many scalps of white men they had killed. Simon could only sit in silent torment. Those men were fellow Americans who had died fighting for freedom.

Frontier Hero

Captain Lernoult thanked the Indians for the scalps and taking a tomahawk from one of the natives pretended to whet it. "You dulled your tomahawks," he said with a grim smile. "Now they are sharp. Go out and dull them again!"

During that winter of 1779 Simon was piecing together bits of information about the Indians, about the strengths and weaknesses of the British forces. He learned the reason why Hamilton had left Detroit just before his arrival as a prisoner. Hamilton had led an army to dislodge the Colonials from Vincennes, and Simon now heard the sad news that the British had recaptured it from General George Rogers Clark.

Simon yearned to escape so that he could carry his information about Detroit to Clark. With his knowledge of the place he was sure that it could be taken. Two other Americans were prisoners there, Jesse Coffer and Nathaniel Bullock. Both were Daniel Boone's men who had been captured by the Indians the previous year and sold to the British. The three, slowly and carefully, began making plans to escape.

Simon spent much time about the trading post, where everyone came and stopped to talk around the wide fireplace. Here he picked up many stray bits of valuable information. Put together they gave him the lay of the land, the forests, hills and prairies of the Wabash country.

He became good friends with John Edgar, the trader, and, being good company, was asked now and then to stay for dinner. He paid for his meals by chopping wood for Mrs. Edgar and doing odd jobs about the place for her.

Captured!

Then one day he mentioned to her quietly that he and his two comrades had enough money for guns and ammunition, but could not buy them openly.

Soon after, Simon went into the trading post and found himself alone with the trader. John Edgar greeted him, then went into the loft and threw down a bundle of moccasins. "Help yourself," he said.

Simon's heart skipped a beat. He knew that Mrs. Edgar had told her husband what he had said about the rifles. Plainly Edgar was helping him.

Simon picked out two pairs of stout moccasins. "I'm very grateful," he said.

"Come to the house after dark," Edgar said softly.

Simon and his two friends went to the Edgar house late that night. Three rifles were handed out to them in the dark, along with pouches of balls and full powder horns. Slipping away cautiously, they hid the equipment in a hollow tree in a swamp, where they had already put a supply of dried meat and parched corn.

Watching their chance, the next night they set off on the route to the west as they had planned. Although they traveled as fast as possible, they were going through swampy land and made slow headway. At dawn they hid out, not stirring again until dark. For two weeks they traveled by night and hid by day, and when their jerky and corn ran out, they lived on raccoon which they shot at night.

Making a wide sweep, they turned south toward the Ohio River. Their moccasins wore out and their feet became bruised and swollen, but they were lucky enough

Frontier Hero

not to see an Indian. For an entire month they traveled through trackless wilderness, guided by Simon's uncanny faculty for finding his way, at night by the stars, the sun by day, or in cloudy weather by the moss on the trees.

Coffer became ill and fell so low in spirits that he said he wished they would run on to some Indians so that he could give himself up to them.

"Ho!" Simon scoffed. "If you had ever been tortured by the red devils you would never let yourself be taken alive."

"Do you really think we will ever make it out safe?" Bullock asked. He was becoming discouraged, too.

"We will reach a white settlement soon," Simon said emphatically. "For seven weeks I saw life and death flash before my eyes. And every time a miracle happened to save me. It made me believe that a special providence is looking out for me."

Later the Indians would speak of him with awe, saying, "The Great Spirit above took him from us little by little—then a little farther and finally took him away altogether."

CHAPTER 7

Dreams of Empire

It was a sultry July day in 1779 when Simon and his two comrades, Jesse Coffer and Nathaniel Bullock, safely reached the falls of the Ohio after their difficult flight. He immediately asked the whereabouts of General George Rogers Clark, and was disappointed to learn that he was many miles west.

Although Simon was exhausted from the hardships and privations of his long trek, he rested only a day before setting off again, this time alone, to find Clark.

"You're crazy to start out again," Jesse Coffer told him. "You'll tempt fate once too often. The settlers say that Injuns are on the prowl around here, and they're in a mean mood."

"I've got to go," Simon insisted. "Clark will want to know about Detroit and the strength of the British there."

He was able to borrow a horse and rode hard until he reached the camp of the general.

Upon first seeing Simon, Clark stared at him as though

Frontier Hero

seeing a ghost. "I heard that the Indians had killed you," he gasped.

Simon said soberly, "They almost did. Several times. But providence protected me. I truly believe that I lead a charmed life. Perhaps fate has some reason for keeping me alive." Then he gave a brief account of his adventures, concluding with his information about Detroit.

"I know the best route," he added, "back to Detroit. The place can be taken with little loss."

Clark shook his head. "I can't risk it," he said. "I can't hope to get any help from either Virginia or Kentucky. The settlers are still smarting from their losses in the campaign against the Indian villages, and my own forces are badly depleted."

Simon started back to Kentucky and on the way he was amazed to discover that, during his captivity and despite all the Indian troubles, several new settlements had sprung up. When he arrived at Harrodsburg the news came that a strong force of British and Indians had invaded Kentucky. They had brought along four cannons and had attacked Martin's and Riddle's stations. Their wood blockhouses could not withstand cannon fire, so the inhabitants were forced to surrender.

As soon as he heard this Simon set out on the trail of the British-Indian force, in order to find out where they were taking the prisoners. He stalked them to a camp on the fork of the Licking River then hurried back to Harrodsburg. He knew that when General Clark heard of the disaster he would seek volunteers to ride to the rescue.

Clark came in to the station soon after and immediately

Dreams of Empire

asked for Simon. The general was not surprised to learn that his daring friend already knew where the prisoners had been taken.

"Simon," General Clark said, "I hereby appoint you as scout for my entire army of volunteers. We move at once!"

The general had only one cannon. Each man furnished his own horse, gun and ammunition, and carried a small supply of jerky and parched corn. The corn ration per day would be but a handful.

Rapidly Simon guided the force of eleven hundred men through the wilderness. They hacked out their own road for the cannon as they traveled. The object was to try to take the enemy by surprise; and as Simon had traveled with Girty through this region, he was able to lead by the best routes and without loss of time.

But arriving at Piqua, where the captives were held, they found the Indians alert for an attack. Though the natives fought like wild men, the deadly fire of the Kentuckians finally sent the survivors fleeing into the woods. The white prisoners were freed, and the town and the cornfield were burned down. The Indians must be taught a lesson, so several more of their villages were attacked and demolished in swift succession.

When Clark decided that the Indians had been sufficiently punished, the army returned to the mouth of the Licking and disbanded, the men returning to their respective settlements. Simon decided to go to Boonesborough and see Daniel Boone. They were kindred spirits, and he wanted to hunt and visit with his friend. He ended up by spending the fall as Boone's guest.

Frontier Hero

Later he went to Lexington, the newest station on the frontier, for he enjoyed making new friends. At this time he was restless, impatient about his future. He still cherished his dream of establishing an empire in the fair land of Kentucky, but he must wait until the war and the Indian troubles were over. Meanwhile he traveled up and down the frontier, getting acquainted with the new settlers, looking over the country and storing in his mind where the choicest sections were.

While at Lexington, Simon met a man who had come from near his boyhood home. Cautiously he asked about the Kenton family. "The Kentons are all well," the man said. "Mark junior is the father of a large family. Several of the other brothers and sisters are married and in homes of their own."

"Do you know the Leachmans?" Simon ventured to ask.

"Oh, yes. I know them well," the man replied.

Simon was afraid to ask his next question for fear he might give away his guilty secret. "How—how about William Leachman?"

"The younger one? He's fine," the stranger replied. "Been married for some time and the father of a fine family."

"You mean—he's alive?"

"Very much so. At least he was when I left there a few months ago."

Simon grew dizzy with relief. Then William wasn't dead! He, Simon, wasn't a murderer. All of these years he had been hiding for a crime he had not committed.

"What did you say your name was?" the man asked.

Dreams of Empire

"Simon Kenton," he replied in a bold voice. He would drop the name of Butler. From now on he would go by his rightful name.

"Simon Kenton!" the man cried. "Your family often spoke of you. They thought you were dead. Why didn't you write?"

"I never learned to read or write," Simon admitted, not wanting to explain the real reason he had disappeared without ever sending word home. "But I sure am going back as soon as I can. I hope to bring them back to this region with me.

The winter he spent in Lexington would go down in history as the "Terrible Winter of 1779–1780." Snow began to fall in the middle of November; from that time to the middle of February Kentucky lay in the grip of ice and sleet.

Kenton and the other settlers found that hunting was no chore, for the animals of the forest were so famished that they came into the settlements. Even buffaloes, their eyes blinded by caked ice, came so close that they could be shot from cabin doors, and wild turkeys fell frozen from the limbs of trees. It kept the settlers busy felling trees and cutting logs for their hungry fireplaces. But the bitter weather also kept the Indians penned within their villages, so that they could not make trouble.

Precious fruit trees, the tender slips of which had been brought all the way from Virginia and Georgia, were frozen. The planting must be done all over again by the disheartened settlers, many of whom wondered why they had left their old homes.

Frontier Hero

Simon himself sometimes wondered this, and at such times homesickness often overwhelmed him. Yet, when he thought the matter over he was glad that he was on his own. Things would not always be as bad as this. Someday the Indian trouble would be over and he would again go exploring for precious land. Someday his dream of founding an empire would come true. Then he would go back to his old home and bring his family back with him.

As soon as the weather moderated sufficiently so that he could travel without danger of freezing to death, Kenton wandered from settlement to settlement getting acquainted. During the lovely spring that finally came he spent most of the time in the region he loved best, around Limestone Creek. He got his old friend Hinkston and several other settlers to help him put up a strong blockhouse at the mouth of the stream. In case of Indian attack, it would serve as a place of refuge for the settlers who were coming into Kentucky by that route.

The Indians and British attacked the house while he was at Boonesborough and burned it down, but Simon only gave up the place for now. He went back again and erected another stronger blockhouse on the site in 1784.

By this time Kentucky was being overrun with surveyors and land agents. Simon had been afraid to take up land under his assumed name of Butler for fear there would be claim trouble later on. But now that he was able to use his real name he chose a beautiful area on the Elkhorn River, put up a log cabin, cleared a plot and planted it to corn.

Settling on his own plot of ground was a heady adven-

Dreams of Empire

ture for Simon. Fired up by the feeling it gave him, he now set out to become one of the largest landholders in Kentucky and Ohio. It became his business to locate plots of land for warrant holders, his payment to be one half of the land he located. In this manner he got ownership of one thousand acres around his old campsite, where the town of Washington, Kentucky, was laid out. The agreement to this big land deal was dated April 28, 1780, and was signed "Simon Kenton. His mark." Simon, now using his rightful last name, still could not write it.

Now that he no longer considered himself a fugitive from justice, the yearning to see his family overcame him and he returned for a visit to Fauquier County, Virginia. Tears came to his eyes when he saw how his parents had aged during the thirteen years since he had run away. But he rejoiced to see that all of his brothers and sisters were alive, all grown and living in their own homes.

He had a great time visiting and reminiscing with the people he had known as children. Then he went to see William Leachman, and at first the visit was somewhat strained. But soon Kenton was telling about all the adventures that had befallen him the past years, and Leachman talked about what had happened at home.

Simon met Mrs. Leachman, who had been his first love when she was Ellen Cummins. She was now stout and matronly, the mother of six children. He chuckled inwardly as he remembered that he had once thought her the most beautiful girl alive.

"William," Simon later said, "if I hadn't feared that I killed you, I would probably have settled down somewhere

Frontier Hero

near here and become a tenant farmer. And I'd still be one. As it stands, however, I own vast acres of rich land. Strange, isn't it? How things work out."

His glowing reports of the fertility and beauty of Kentucky so enthused his entire family that they all decided to go back with him and settle there. It gave him great pleasure to tell them that he had land enough for all of them. The whole family would be together, he said, and he never wanted to be separated from them again.

The Kenton party traveled to Redstone Fort on horseback, and stayed there long enough to build rafts. While engaged in this work the father was overcome by what was evidently a heart attack and died suddenly. He was buried near there on the bank of the Monongahela.

The death of his eighty-three-year-old father saddened Simon, but he was thankful that he would be able to take care of his mother and the rest of the family. They floated down the river to the falls of the Ohio, then made their way to Simon's station on Salt River. Without exception they were tremendously impressed by the richness and beauty of the land. Simon, they agreed, had not told half the wonders of it. Altogether they made up quite a little settlement of their own, after Simon's brothers and the husbands of his sisters had erected cabins. They numbered forty-one people including several Negro servants, and twelve of the group were capable of fighting should Indians attack.

The first cabins were purposely not very elaborate, for time was short as it was nearly winter. Besides, Kenton still had his heart set on a larger, better settlement in the Limestone region. As he helped his relatives with the building of their rude shelters his spirits soared; people of his own blood were settling this fair land, his land and theirs.

Now there were to be heard women's songs and children's laughter. The Salt River station hummed with activity. Within the cabins, beds were no longer simple mats of dried leaves. They were real beds of framework, and covered with patchwork quilts from Virginia rather than coarse buffalo robes. There were pots and kettles in which to cook a delicious meal from the game which Simon brought in, rather than thin strips of meat twisted around a ramrod to be half-smoked and half-charred over a campfire.

He showed his people how to make a hominy stump by cutting and burning out a hollow in a tree stump. In this, parched corn was poured and pounded to coarse particles. This method was similar to the one the Indians used for making their corn meal, except that they used a hollowed-out stone. For finer corn meal the settlers made a woodman's sieve—a deerskin stretched over a willow hoop and punched full of holes with a red-hot fork. The hominy grits were then sifted through this crude strainer.

Corn would be the main crop raised by the settlers for many years, for it was a most versatile food. The meal mixed with water and salt and cooked on slabs before the fire made a nourishing pone or bread. Parched corn was always carried by the settlers when they went Indian fighting or exploring. Plain boiled cornmeal mush was a standard dish, and mixed with raccoon, opossum or bear fat was considered a luxury.

Frontier Hero

When he had his Salt River settlements well established, Simon went back in January to his Limestone site. There he located and surveyed more land for himself and for the colonists he knew would come the next spring. The Indians had not made any attacks since Clark's campaign of 1782, but they were active in stealing horses and killing cattle whenever they had a chance. So prevalent grew Indian signs along the frontier that Simon thought it wiser to engage a group to help with the job of surveying. As guide and scout, he always led off the march. The surveyors, chain carriers and markermen followed in line, with the cook bringing up the rear.

While Kenton was surveying he heard that a party of Indians had massacred a party of campers. The tragedy caused Simon to go ahead with the plan he had kept in mind. And this was when he rebuilt the blockhouse at the mouth of Limsetone Creek. Built on a hill, from this vantage point Kenton could scan the country on two sides and watch the river to see if Indians, or settlers, were approaching.

During 1785 twenty families moved in and built cabins in a hollow square around Simon's blockhouse. Strangely enough, or perhaps because of its imposing strength, the place was never attacked or raided by Indians, and the blockhouse stood for many years on the northern frontier of Kentucky. Because of the pure spring gushing from the hillside and the fertile land around, it was an ideal location. Later Kenton's Station would be renamed Maysville, then Washington. Within five years it would boast 119 cabins.

Dreams of Empire

Meetinghouses were built at various settlements or stations, and the Reverend William Wood became the roving preacher for the infant villages. Later the Reverend Robert Finley came to Washington. His son James would write about Simon Kenton in his autobiography:

> That truly great adventurer was truly the master spirit of the time in that region of the country. He was looked upon by all as the great defender of the inhabitants, always on the alert, and ready to fly at a moment's warning to the place of danger for the protection of the scattered families in the wilderness. . . . He was regarded as the prince of pioneers in this region of the country and he was the teacher and captain of all the young boys in those parts."

At first Kenton had given large plots of land to his relatives; later he began to sell land that he had located and surveyed. Now the settlers were erecting larger and more permanent cabins, but without windows, for through these Indians might enter. The doors were thick and heavy and at night were firmly barred. No one ever opened his door in the morning until he had first climbed a ladder into the loft, and peered through the cracks to make sure that no Indians were lurking about.

The cabins had dirt floors at first, for puncheons—logs split down the center—were difficult to hew by hand. Their wide fireplaces, for cooking and heat, were built of "cats and clay"—small branches mixed with the down from cattails and mud. This material was surprisingly fireproof. When the Indians burned a cabin with such a fireplace the chimney stood tall over the ruins.

After the log cabin had been raised and the family was living in it the chinking began. Slowly the cracks between the logs were filled with slabs of wood of any size then daubed with clay. When the chinking was finished the cabin was snug and weatherproof.

While the building was going on, the acres of canebrakes were being cleared and gardens prepared. Beans, pumpkins, cabbages, turnips, potatoes and the mainstay, corn, were planted. The forests provided a wealth of game animals and birds, and the settlers usually lived well.

At Limestone the year after Kenton's Station was built, a rude mill was put up in which the settlers could have their corn ground into meal. Wheat flour was coming down the river now, but few settlers could afford it for it cost ten dollars a barrel.

Kenton had not been long at his station before an old friend appeared, Pierre Druillard, who had once saved his life. It was he who had persuaded the Shawnee, who held Simon prisoner, to let him take Kenton to Detroit to be interviewed by the British.

Now, as Kenton kindly put it, Druillard had "become unfortunate." A weakness for hard liquor beset him and for fourteen years, until Pierre's death, Kenton supported him and his family.

Simon's son later wrote:

> He supported Druillard during all those years of idleness and intemperance and always treated him with the

utmost kindness and respect—would always have him sit at his right hand at table and give him the best he had and wait on him first. He gave him a horse to ride and dressed him in broadcloth.

Druillard's son, George, grew up at Kenton's Station and adopted Kenton as his hero to pattern himself after. Later, George Druillard would go to the Pacific with Lewis and Clark after he "had a parting frolic at Kenton's."

In the spring of 1786 the Indians once again took up the war trail. They drove off nearly all of the horses at Limestone and Licking and waylaid and killed two men on the way to prayer meeting.

Soon after that a Dutchman, John Kinsualla, was seized one night while out looking for his cows. Then George Rogers Clark's son, Robert, and a Negro boy were taken captive.

At this time Kenton mustered a group of men to fight with him. He did this "on his own hook," an expression he often used. They called themselves "Kenton's Boys" and pledged themselves to be ready at a minute's notice to follow Simon wherever he led them. No pay and no supplies were given them; each man furnished his own mount, food and ammunition.

Whenever an Indian alarm was sounded, each man would saddle his horse, take his bullets and powder horn, and sally forth to "give the Indians a teach." For eight years "Kenton's Boys" defended the frontier, and a band of heroes like them has seldom been known before or since.

Frontier Hero

Finally as a result of continuing raids on the frontier, Benjamin Logan's Campaigners of 1786 were mustered. All through the end of summer, boats, ammunition and provisions were collected. Then Logan's forces met at Limestone and were joined by Kenton's Boys. The women in the nearby stations stayed up an entire night parching corn, making jerky and cooking journey cake.

The crossing of the Ohio by the Campaigners took a night and a day, the men landing at Eagle Creek. Then they marched through an opening in the hills which from that day on would be known as Logan's Gap. It was a place which had painful memories for Simon, for it was here that he had been captured by the Shawnee. But the route was one which he knew well, and he was able to guide the men straight to the Indian village in six days of hard traveling.

Early in the morning of October 5 a man deserted and ran ahead to Machachak, warning the Indians of the coming of the whites. Learning this, Logan ordered a forced march, with half his force to attack Machachak. He sent Kenton and his "Boys," including Daniel Boone, to attack Moluntha's Town. However, by the time they came up, most of the warriors had fled to the thickets, swamps and high grass of the prairies.

Simon and his men were ready to burn the village when they saw something. Hanging on a stick thrust in the ground was a grim memento—the scalp of a Negro.

Simon shook his head sadly. "I'm afeared," he said, "that Robert has met the same fate. I was hoping for General Clark's sake that we would be able to rescue his son."

Dreams of Empire

Before they applied the torch to the cabins, they examined each one for some sign of prisoners. In one they found cards bearing the name of Robert Clark and his parents and brothers and sisters.

Seeing these, Simon said, "Maybe—just maybe—there is hope for Robert after all." But they found no other signs of the young prisoner.

Before this punitive raid was over Simon and his boys took forty prisoners. They were taken back to Kenton's Station and placed in the stockade to be used in ransoming the white prisoners.

CHAPTER 8

Kenton and His "Boys"

After Kenton had settled his family at his station and had provided them with generous plots of land he received a message. Mrs. Dowden, the sister of William Kenton's wife, was coming to Kentucky to be near the only kin she had left. Her husband had died recently, leaving her with four children to rear.

Simon took extra horses and rode to Limestone, four miles away, to meet them when they landed. He was amused and pleased by the way the oldest child, fourteen-year-old Martha, bustled around, taking care of the younger children. She had a way of doing what needed to be done, capably and without being told.

"In a few years," Simon told her, "you will make some settler a good wife."

"Do you have a wife, Mr. Kenton?" she asked.

"No," he replied, "I'm a dyed-in-the-wool bachelor."

At the time he had no thought of marriage; but he saw a good deal of the Dowden family while he helped erect their cabin. The widow on occasion asked his advice or assistance, and he made it a point to keep the little family supplied with meat. The years sped by and Martha Dowden was seventeen. Almost overnight it seemed that she had changed from a girl into a woman. When Simon realized the miracle which had taken place, he suddenly knew that he was in love with Martha and wanted to marry her.

He asked the widow Dowden if he might court her oldest daughter.

"I could not ask for a finer son-in-law," she replied, "nor a better husband for my Martha. Despite the difference in your ages, I don't consider the gap too great at all. You are only thirty-two and she is going on eighteen. She is lucky that the foremost hero of the frontier wants her as wife."

He took Martha walking down the trail by the river one Sunday afternoon and asked her if she would consider marrying him.

To his surprise she answered, "I've been considering it for some time. I thought, though, that I'd have to do the proposing, you were so slow about it."

"You mean—that you're accepting me?" He stopped still in the path.

"I've loved you since the first moment I saw you."

Then they were in each others arms and Martha promised to marry him before the fields were tilled.

During the winter Simon worked hard bringing in game for the twenty-two families now settled at his station. He was also putting a puncheon floor in his own cabin, so that Martha would have all the comforts he was able to provide.

Frontier Hero

A Baptist minister had come to live at Kenton's Station, and on February 17, 1787, Simon Kenton and Martha Dowden were married by Parson Wood. The wedding took place at the Dowden cabin, the first such celebration to take place at Kenton's Station.

A year later Simon's first child, named after his dearly beloved sister Nancy, was born. But marriage did not keep Simon at home, for the safety of the colonists depended upon his vigilance. Even when the Indians were quiet it was assumed that they were planning trouble, so Kenton and his "Boys" kept the redskins painfully aware that the white men were alert."

Within three months after his marriage Simon took a handful of his "Boys" and went out on a scouting expedition. After traveling a few miles Kenton saw Indian signs, and with three of his men crept close to their village. He heard the Shawnee talking about some scouts they had sent to spy upon the whites, just as another group came in with horses stolen from the settlements.

Simon hurried back to Limestone and sent out the message that big Indian trouble was brewing, advising that an expedition be launched against the savages to discourage them from attacking. In the spring some two hundred men came in from the various settlements in response to Kenton's call. Colonel Robert Todd was chosen as commander, Kenton as usual as guide.

They marched swiftly to Paint Creek, the camp to which the Indians had brought the stolen horses, and took this small band without a struggle. The handful of prisoners were persuaded to tell Simon of a larger camp up-

Kenton and His "Boys"

stream about half a day's march. There the white men found a supply of rawhide halters and leading ropes; evidently a horse-stealing expedition was being planned.

Kenton set out for the village with a small detachment of men, but traveled so fast that the main body was left far behind. When he got within sight of the Indians he was forced to send back word that the redskins far outnumbered him; he would wait until the others came up to him. The two parties joined at dawn and attacked the village, only to find but a few old men, women and children there. Kenton's party went on to other camps, finding them also deserted by warriors but taking as prisoners a number of women and a few old men. These the settlers would hold for ransoming the white prisoners the Indians had.

The pressure was on the savages, and they knew it. A group of sixty Shawnee in ceremonial war paint soon came to Washington, Kentucky, to sue for peace and exchange prisoners. The Limestone Treaty was agreed upon.

Among others, the Dutchman, John Kinsualla, was exchanged. But the biggest surprise was the return of George Rogers Clark's son, Robert. He had an exciting story to tell. After his capture he had been adopted by one of the squaws. Then during Logan's campaign she had hidden him to prevent his being killed in revenge for the death of one of the chiefs. General Clark was beside himself with happiness, and grateful to Simon Kenton.

The settlers killed a beef and barbecued it to celebrate the signing of the peace, while the Indians danced to the

Frontier Hero

pounding of their drums. The feasting and a celebration, however, were held across the Ohio River from Limestone; and the savages were required to stack their guns.

The Shawnee departed in good spirits because they had got some of their people back. But the Kentuckians had also, and in addition many of their stolen horses. The Indians had no intention of keeping their part of the treaty. They continued to steal horses and attack settlements whenever the mood seized them.

Kenton understood Indians and their sudden whims and never for an instant relaxed his vigilance. In 1789 he was out with a party of his own surveyors and practiced his usual caution. At night he was very careful in selecting a campsite near a creek. Then to keep the place from being discovered he waded half a mile down the creek bottom, crossed the stream and went up the same distance on the other side. Crossing back there again to his camp, he had left a confusing double trail on each side of the creek.

Spencer Record and Tobias Woods were out hunting buffalo and came upon the trail left by Kenton. Fearing this might be Indian sign they tightened their leggings and moccasins for running, but stealthily followed the trail. At the second crossing they were sighted by Kenton's lookout, who ran back to camp reporting two "Indians" nearby. The two hunters saw a shadowy figure running back to camp and immediately climbed into trees to hide, expecting to see redskins rush out.

"Show yourselves or be shot!" a familiar voice shouted.

"Simon Kenton!" Woods cried. "Don't shoot! We are Woods and Record." They climbed down to be greeted

Kenton and His "Boys"

by Kenton and offered a dollar a day to stay and work for him.

In spite of the fact that Indian troubles were not over, many settler wagons were moving over the new road leading from Limestone to the Blue Licks. And down the Ohio were coming numerous vessels called Kentucky flatboats or arks. These were enormous scows made of four-inch planks, with a cabin in the center extending the entire width of the craft.

The flatboats were large enough to carry a family, a wagon, a team of horses and a cow, as well as supplies for a long journey downstream.

They were also floating forts, shaped like huge boxes, with portholes for guns. On the flat roofs of the cabins could be carried plows, wagons and a haystack for the livestock. But the animals had to be penned inside.

The flatboats brought settlers looking for new homes—settlers who came from the East with furniture, cooking equipment and prized family possessions.

Many relatives and friends flocked to the shore to meet the newcomers and guide them to settlements. The frontier echoed to the sound of saw and axe, the shouting of men, and the gentler voices of women and children.

Despite Simon's vigilance there were several Indian attacks. Thomas Kelsey and his partner of Kenton's Station were moving a family of new settlers on pack horses. That night as they sat around the campfire three Indians fired at them from the bushes, killing one man and wounding Kelsey. His partner ran to Kenton's Station and told Simon what had happened. Immediately Kenton and sev-

Frontier Hero

eral of his "Boys" set out on the trail. They caught up with the redskins just as they were starting to cross the Ohio, and shot them on the spot. It was only by such quick reprisals as this that Kenton was able to hold the Indians in check. They knew that any raid would promptly be punished.

By this time Kenton's domain comprised many thousands of acres. He was always generous with his land, settling every member of his own family on desirable sites without charge, and selling plots to others for reasonable sums. He had no great desire for money, but took great pride in the ownership of a vast area of rich and beautiful land.

One day a man came from Virginia with a warrant for a large area which he was about to place on Simon's land. At this terrible affront one of those gigantic rages of which he was capable flared up in Kenton. Seizing a heavy stick, Kenton rushed at the man and beat him severely. The man tried to escape but Simon followed wherever he attempted to run. The would-be land thief was badly bruised all over before Simon gave up teaching him a lesson, and he made no more attempts to take over any of Kenton's precious land.

Now, due to Kenton's enormous labors, the northern frontier of Kentucky was no longer a wilderness. His region was Mason County, with half a dozen towns and a dozen stations built around the core of his own. Through Simon's unflagging alertness and zeal the port of Limestone had been made safe, and settlers' flatboats and arks clogged its shores. Fort Washington was built from the timbers

Kenton and His "Boys"

of those same craft. By 1789 there were twenty thousand people in Kentucky. Within another four years there would be over seventy thousand, and the immigration had just begun.

Although Mason County now had its own military organization, Kenton was still the chief scout of any punitive expedition which set out. He was relied upon more than ever to smell out any trouble the Indians were about to incite. And he had only to blow upon his horn to bring his "Boys" on the run from all surrounding settlements. He could rely on them for instant action, and many times it was this quick action which saved lives of the settlers. The Indians held Simon Kenton in great awe, and his reputation was a strong force in protecting the frontier.

In the spring of 1790, however, Simon's method of defending the frontier was dealt a crashing blow. Orders came from a Mason County official that no party "under any pretense whatever shall enter the Territory of the United States or of any Indian tribe."

This order, had the Kentuckians obeyed it, would have left the settlers powerless to make reprisals or to recapture stolen horses or captives. Nor could they even have scouted for signs that an Indian war party was on its way to the towns. The settlers were forbidden to cross the Ohio, even if they were attacked.

Early in April, Black Snake and a band of warriors topped a series of raids by taking John May's boat on the Ohio shore. Ignoring the order, Kenton quickly led a party who killed four Indians. The depredations ceased for several months. Then early in the fall James Livingston was captured while on his way from Lexington to Limestone with several wagons of supplies. A group of Shawnee waylaid this train, killed Livingston's two companions and carried him off as a captive.

News of this attack interrupted the first wedding to take place at May's Lick. However, all of the male guests had come armed. Without waiting for the wedding ceremony they mounted their horses and galloped off with Simon Kenton. He quickly found the trail and led his men to the Ohio River, and again ignored that order. They crossed the river, marched to the Bullskin and found where the Indians had camped.

Warned of the approach of Kenton's party the Shawnee had quickly fled, leaving behind their blankets and other supplies. Kenton was after them at once and found that they had not gone far before they had divided into three parties. He stood at the point where the trail separated and all of his men looked at him, waiting for his decision. He did not have enough men to send in all three directions so he must try to figure out which party had Livingston. He let his mind "send out feelers," as he explained it, then chose the central trail to follow.

After his party had gone about two miles the trail split in two and once more he must make the decision which party to follow. Frowning, Simon studied the trails. There was nothing to indicate on which trail the captive had been taken, but Simon chose the right-hand one. They traveled until dark, then camped without fire.

At daybreak Kenton and his party took up the trail once more. Soon they heard the Indians shouting, which was

Kenton and His "Boys"

their habit after breaking camp and was evidence that they now considered themselves safe from pursuit.

Kenton's men had followed the natives for about two miles when they came to a place where there was a great deal of fallen timber. New tree growth made a screen there, but as it thinned out Simon spied the Indians ahead of them only a short distance. There were four of them with Livingston, who had been dressed to look like an Indian. Hearing the white men approach, the Indians started to run. Simon gave the signal to fire. The Indians fell.

At the sound of the shots Livingston turned and raised his hands in the air. "Wagon. My wagon!" he shouted in his excitement. What he meant was that he was the man of the wagon train who had been captured. He feared he would be shot as an Indian because of his garb.

When Kenton's party came up, Livingston said, "Before you arrived, I thought that my captors were running from other Indians. I still can't believe that a rescue party could move so quickly. Especially since there were five trails to choose from. How did you know which trail to follow?"

Simon shrugged. "Just instinct, I reckon," he said. "I don't know how I knew, but it was like something pulling me along the trail I took."

During the winter of 1790–1791 the Indians were quiet, and Simon had time to rest from defense of the border. On December 11, his second child, John, was born. His daughter, Nancy, was a little over two years old at the time. It made Simon's Christmas a merry one to have two little ones in the family.

The settlements continued to increase about Limestone. Nathaniel Massie, who had explored and surveyed with Kenton for several years, announced his new settlement named Manchester, opposite the lower of Three Islands. He promised to each of the twenty-five first settlers of his new town a lot and one hundred acres of land. About thirty families settled there with him.

In order to protect the border General Scott ordered two officers and sixteen soldiers to range along the frontier. These men were all Kenton's "Boys" and had been well trained by him. They did their work well, but the job was too big for them.

During the years 1789 to 1791 Simon was not engaged in any battles with the Indians, but he did go out to scout now and then to let them know that he was still alert. He was rich in land and livestock, and where his blockhouse had once stood he now built a brick house for his family. It was the finest home on the frontier. And as Simon was the soul of hospitality there were usually guests at his home.

With the coming of the spring of 1791 Indian attacks on boats coming down the Ohio grew more frequent and savage. Obviously the little army ordered out by General Scott was not sufficient to cope with this problem, or lacked the aggressive leadership needed to impress the Indians. Something must be done.

CHAPTER 9

Work Well Done

In the spring of 1792 the Indian attacks increased along the Ohio River and among the Kentucky settlements. The small corps appointed by the government had proved inadequate to control the hostiles. After a particularly daring raid by Tecumseh's warriors Kenton decided to take matters into his own hands and do something "on his own hook."

Simon sent runners speeding to the nearby settlements with the alarm, and thirty-seven of his picked men hurried to his side. The Indians had moved toward the head of the Little Miami but Kenton soon picked up the trail. When he came near the east fork of the stream he heard a bell in the distance. Most of the horses stolen from the settlers wore bells.

Simon halted his party and took Cornelius Washburn and three other members to scout ahead. They were stalking along the trail, silent as shadows, when suddenly Simon saw an Indian riding toward him. The bell sound came from the redskin's horse. Simon knew that both

Frontier Hero

Indians and white men sometimes hunted with bells on their horses. Deer were not alarmed by the noise and would often pause to locate the strange sound and become easy prey.

Kenton signaled for his men to conceal themselves and for Washburn to shoot the savage when he came near enough. As the enemy rode in to an open space Simon shouted "Halloo!"

The Indian stopped his horse and looked around in alarm. Washburn fired and the Indian fell. Kenton and his scouts then hurried back to the main party to discuss what to do. It was certain that this redskin was not alone or his companions far away.

After the situation had been talked over, Simon said, "I'm sure we're on the trail of the raiding varmints and that they are a large party. They may not be far away so we must be careful. Washburn and I will scout ahead. The rest of you follow us quietly."

Soon Kenton and his partner heard the faint sound of many bells about a quarter of a mile ahead and doubled back to tell the rest of the party.

"The bell sounds are scattered," Simon explained, "like horses grazing here and there. This must be their main camp."

With the stealthy tread of panthers, the two men followed the trail until they came within view of many tepees. The village stretched well around into the forest, and Kenton guessed that the number of warriors there must be at least five times his own force. But in spite of the

Work Well Done

superiority of the Indians it was decided to attack them after dark.

Simon divided his party into little sections of four men each. "Each unit will attack a tepee," he ordered. "We strike at midnight. By then the enemy should be asleep. That will allow us, if they counterattack, to make our getaway in the dark."

So quiet was their approach that they were within a few steps from the tepees when Simon yelled the signal. Leaning forward, Kenton's men fired a deadly volley at the astonished warriors as they jumped from their sleeping robes and tried to escape.

Kenton did not have enough men to attack more than about half of the lodges but they routed the enemy. However, unsuspected by the whites another band of Indians was camped farther down the creek and they came rushing up to rescue Tecumseh's defeated warriors. Kenton saw then that he would be surrounded by superior forces and shouted for his men to retreat.

Only two of the white men were killed, and at least thirty Indians had been slain and twice that number wounded. Though Kenton's party had not recovered any stolen horses, the expedition was counted a huge success, and it would be many moons before the Indians dared to raid again. However, the increase of settlers in Kentucky continued to make the redskins angry and fearful that their favorite hunting ground was being ruined.

Simon's station in Mason County was filling up especially fast, and he kept scouts out constantly ranging the area to give notice of impending Indian attacks. And it

Frontier Hero

was known along the whole Kentucky frontier that if any place were hit by hostiles Kenton would take quick action to punish them.

Simon wanted to settle down and devote more time to his family, but the thing of utmost importance now was to protect the rapidly expanding settlements.

"Someday, Martha," he said as he was filling a pouch with parched corn and maple sugar for a scouting journey, "the frontier will be civilized. Then I can spend more time at home with you and the little ones. I can't blame the Injuns for being mad about their territory being taken over by the whites, but this land is fertile. It shouldn't go to waste. It should be cultivated. The whites need the land and will till the soil—the Injuns won't. So," he sighed, "we will have to fight for it."

"You are so reckless," she said. "Must you always be out in the lead?"

"I'm the scout and leader of my men," he said. "I must lead. But don't worry, my dear. Fate has always protected me."

"God has protected you," she corrected him gently. "You are in my prayers constantly."

Simon continued to be the main force in guarding the frontier which he had fathered, and the year of 1793 would be a busy one for him and his men.

Good news reached Simon that summer. General Anthony Wayne had been made commander-in-chief of the regular army and was coming down the Ohio to establish peace in Kentucky. He called for reinforcements from

Work Well Done

Kentuckians, and Kenton and his Boys were the first to respond. Simon suggested that his men, with their vast experience, act as scouts, and Wayne gladly accepted his proposal. Kenton, however, insisted that he be allowed to pick the volunteers for this force himself. Wayne made him a major to head his band of one hundred scouts; he was also to act as chief guide for the entire army.

Kenton's picked body of men performed more and better service than any other division in Wayne's army. Kenton was called upon to share in all councils and meetings of the campaign and was listened to with great respect. His trained men brought in scores of prisoners and in battle slew many enemies. They were without rival in the army and sought to make each expedition outdo the one which had preceded it. Although they were considered "lucky" because they came out unharmed from so many desperate encounters, Simon never lost his sense of caution. It was that same sense which gave him and his men their luck.

Fort Greenville was built. Then, since the season was far advanced, Wayne decided to suspend his expeditions and build Fort Recovery. Kenton grew impatient of Wayne's slow tactics. He thought that the army ought to be driving out the Indians instead of building forts. There was another major with Wayne, "Wild Man" McMahon of the regulars, as courageous as Kenton and just as impatient of inaction.

General Wayne heard of their discontent and consented to their taking three hundred men out to find and attack hostiles. This contingent pushed forward until it was near the mouth of the Auglaize, close to Fort Defiance, where there was Indian sign. Finally the scouts found many trails coming from different directions and all converging upon the same center.

McMahon was for attacking without delay. Kenton, who had more experience, told him that the sign indicated a tremendous gathering of Indians. He suggested caution, and possible retreat.

McMahon said, "I would not think of retreating without a fight."

"Such action is unwise," Simon pointed out. "We do not know their numbers. If you're determined to fight I'll support you. But let's discuss it."

Nothing was decided that night. After sleeping on the matter, McMahon decided that Kenton was wiser in Indian fighting than he, and bowed to his better judgment. Several officers laughed at them when they returned without having given battle, but Wayne commended them upon their sound decision.

Kenton stayed at Greenville until winter, when he became ill. As soon as he was able to travel again he took his discharge and returned home.

So he missed being with Wayne in 1794 at the Battle of Fallen Timbers, which marked the end of the twenty-year war with the Indians. The Treaty of Greenville ended Kenton's battles with the Indians; but it marked the beginning of many legal battles for land.

Now began for him a new and different way of life. To his children Nancy and John had been added Simon junior. In 1795, his daughter Sarah was born. He was the head of the clan, a benign patriarch. His brothers, John and

Work Well Done

William, had finally come to Kentucky. Now his entire family surrounded him. He had numerous slaves, many horses and tenant farmers to raise his crops.

At all times he kept open house and set a bountiful table at which anyone was welcome. His corn cribs were full and running over. Newcomers, travelers or the needy were welcome to help themselves, and Simon grandly refused payment. "Have you money to pay for it?" he would say. "Then go and buy of those who have to sell. Mine is not for sale, but for use and to bestow upon the needy and newcomers without money. There are my cribs filled with plenty. Go and shell as much as you need."

His generosity was so great that his tenants took advantage of him. At harvest time they put his share in his cribs, but when their supplies grew short they would without permission take as much of Kenton's as they needed. Such management made farming unprofitable for him.

It was with all he owned as it was with his corn; he shared everything he had with his neighbors. He gave the fine lands about Washington away free to anyone who would farm them. He owned a trading post at Washington stocked with guns, ammunition, knives, farming implements, blankets, food, clothing, shoes and such merchandise. He gave unlimited credit to anyone who came for supplies, and as a result there was little profit in this business. But Simon had little use for money. He was, however, "land crazy." It seemed that he could not get and own enough acres to satisfy him, although after he had it he gave the land away freely.

He encouraged settlers, yet the country was getting too

civilized and "crowded" to suit him; he was often restless and vaguely dissatisfied. Being "settled down" was new to him and a situation far too inactive for his nature.

Packet boats were traveling regularly upriver from Cincinnati to Pittsburgh, and mail was coming frequently from Wheeling. Zane's Trace had been cut from Wheeling to Limestone, linking the East and the West. The river was now covered with all sorts of vessels—flatboats, keelboats, arks and canoes. Not only settlers were flooding in, but merchandise to provision them: flour, bacon, sugar, coffee, furniture, iron, pottery and many other articles of civilized living.

Simon became so busy with land deals, trading and every kind of business that he had to get a secretary. He asked Israel Donalson, Kentucky's first schoolteacher, to come to Limestone and act in handling his papers and deeds.

Donalson found himself lost in a "maze of confusion." He later said that Kenton was "a man of noble character, entirely illiterate," although Simon had learned to scrawl two words, which by a stretch of imagination might be read as "Simon Kenton."

The former schoolteacher also wrote:

> He had an extraordinary memory; he once called upon me to file his papers. When I went to his house he had two drawers of an old-fashioned file full of papers and would come and stand by me, and when I picked up a paper, before opening it he would tell me what it was.
>
> The man's memory for visual details was extraordinary. Although he could not read any paper, he could select any one he wanted out of any number in a pocket, by its

Work Well Done

shape or some peculiarity in its appearance, and give its gist before it was read to him for the purpose of refreshing his mind. ...

Simon's remarkable memory was well known. Many men spoke of his phenomenal faculty for mastering the detailed physical geography of any region over which he had passed.

Because of the lack of any system of filing on landholdings, beautiful Kentucky was literally shingled with overlapping patents, leading to interminable lawsuits. Simon Kenton had frequently been employed as a locator, and he had taken as pay a part interest in such land.

Simon's first holding entry was on the Elkhorn River. But later on, a man named McConnell filed on the same piece of land. Simon took the matter to court in August 1788. Being the first case of its kind, it became famous, for upon its decision would hinge the homes and farms of other pioneers.

Justice, however, moved slowly in those days, and it was ten years before it was finally decided in Kenton's favor. McConnell appealed the decision, and it was five more years before the Court of Appeals handed down a decree in Kenton's favor "confirmed and unaltered." Had the case gone against him the land of nearly every pioneer in Kentucky would have been endangered, and many homes would have been taken away from those who had fought for Kentucky during the first three years of its settlement.

During his legal battles he met Judge Jacob Burnett, who became a lifetime friend. The judge wrote of him after a visit,

Frontier Hero

He was then possessed of a large estate. And a more generous, kindhearted man did not inhabit the Earth. His door was always open. Neither stranger nor friend ever found it shut and the latch string pulled in. Travelers of every grade were received with kindness, treated with hospitality and pressed to stay.

At that time Simon's home was filled with newly arrived relatives, Stephen Jarboe from Maryland with his wife and children. But the happy Kentucky days were nearly over. While Simon was away from home in December 1796, disaster struck the "fine brick house." The then pregnant Mrs. Martha Kenton was sleeping in a downstairs room. A piece of burning wood from an upstairs fireplace rolled from the hearth, burned slowly through the floor and fell flaming on her bed. She was so badly burned that her premature baby and she died.

The Jarboes stayed with Simon to care for his four motherless children. The house had been gutted by the fire, but the neighbors came and helped Simon and Stephen Jarboe build a log cabin.

The oldest Jarboe daughter, Elizabeth, was a black-haired, blue-eyed beauty, vivacious and fun-loving. Simon thought that she would marry Reuben Clark, who was courting her.

When the terrible grief over Martha's tragic death had diminished somewhat, Simon gradually became aware of Elizabeth's intelligence and gaiety. She had all of the education available to girls of that day and was teaching Simon's Nancy and John to read and write. She also took care of all four of his children.

Work Well Done

One day after she had finished telling his children a bedtime story, Simon said, "You are good to my children. Why, Elizabeth?"

"Because I love them dearly."

There was a long silence, then Simon said, "And I have learned to love you dearly, Elizabeth. Will you marry me?"

She looked up at him archly. "I was wondering if you would ever ask me. Of course, I'll be proud to be your wife, Simon."

Leaving his four children in the care of the Jarboes, Simon took his bride on a unique honeymoon. He still had the yen to explore and he wanted to see what Missouri looked like. Their only way to travel through this new frontier was by raft and pack horse. Kentucky was becoming too crowded for him. The game had moved to this outland "where man had not yet come to spoil Nature's largess."

He still had the hunger for land, but all of the choicest acres in Kentucky had been taken. With the burning of his home and the death of his first wife, a break had come in his life. He had decided to move to Ohio, where the chances were brightest in the new field of land speculation; when all of the choice land in Ohio should be entered, there was all of Missouri. Upon his return from his honeymoon he moved to Cincinnati where he remained until the birth of his daughter Matilda, on January 23, 1799.

Thus, twenty-eight years after he came to the country of the cane lands, one of the first white men there, and just when life in Kentucky was becoming comfortable, he

Frontier Hero

moved out on a new trail. Many of his relatives and friends would follow him on his new migration. The wilderness was conquered by men like Kenton and Daniel Boone, men who must always move on looking for new frontiers, for more "elbow room."

CHAPTER 10

"On His Own Hook"

The trail which Kenton cut through the wilderness to his new land in Ohio would be called Kenton's Trace, and the settlers who followed him over it traveled on horseback or on foot. Later his trace would become a wagon road. Simon rode at the head of his little colony of relatives, friends and slaves, flanked by John and Archibald Dowden. These were his nephews, whom he had trained as his "Boys" and who were as alert as Simon himself in reading Indian signs. The white settlers were again on their way to take possession of Indian country.

The place he had picked for his new home was a beautiful spot in Ohio, a rolling hill in the midst of a great prairie, skirted by groves of wild cherry, plum and crab. It was graced with a gushing spring so fine that it became a well-known camping ground for wagons and movers coming later to Ohio. Here he staked out a thousand-acre tract, four miles north of where Springfield would be located.

Simon always called his wife "Betsey." He would come

Frontier Hero

home from his frequent, mysterious wanderings and sit down before the fire as though he had only been on a visit to the neighbors. His invariable greeting, given in his soft voice, was "Well with thee, Betsey?"

"It is well with me, Simon," was her usual response. She did not chide him about his absences, for she realized that he was a strange man who must have his periods of solitude. Between the two was a deep and abiding understanding. She allowed him to come and go as he pleased, knowing that otherwise he would have been miserable. She did not even ask where he had been, but waited patiently for the mood to come upon him, when he would voluntarily tell about his trip. To her he was a great man. She took down many of Simon's dictated recollections, and it was due to her that they were recorded for posterity.

The men worked hard through the summer in the new settlement, building fourteen cabins and a blockhouse for protection from the Indians. Kenton dropped in one night to see how William Owen was coming with his work.

Much disturbed, Owen said, "A band of Indians has set up camp only about two hundred yards away. I don't like the looks of it. Two men who acted as traders among the Indians were present and one of them said, 'I don't believe the redskins are naturally ferocious. Any of us would fight if our homes were being taken from us.'"

Simon gave a derisive snort. "I never had any schooling, but I had a good education in Indian warfare and I'm a graduate of their school of torture. The lessons my cruel teachers taught me are engraved on my memory and my body." He inclined his head. "Here, William, feel the

"On His Own Hook"

dents on my skull left by blows from a pipe tomahawk."

"By gar!" William exclaimed. "It's a wonder that they didn't crack your skull wide open."

Simon nodded and went on, "In spite of what I've suffered from the Injuns, I feel sorry for them. As you say, this is their homeland. But civilization must in time win out. The Injuns will have to accept it, and we must fight them until they learn the lesson."

Thinking that all was well with the Owen family, Simon returned to his home. The next morning he returned to the Owen cabin to borrow an axe. "How are you, Jinney?" he said as he walked in. Then he stopped in his tracks for the room was a shambles.

"What happened?" he cried.

Sobbing and still quivering with fright, Mrs. Owen said, "Last night the Cherokee, Billy George, came here. He was very drunk. Trader Whittlesey took his arm and tried to lead him outside. But Billy George stabbed Whittlesey. My husband and trader Felix then forced Billy outside and tied him to a tree. He got away, but they caught him again and tied him up and whipped him...."

"Where are the men now?" Kenton asked.

"They took Billy to Chief Wolf to demand that he be punished."

Kenton turned on his heel and hurried to the Indian camp to take part in the conference. He found Owen and the two traders in Chief Wolf's lodge. Billy George was opposite the chief who motioned to Simon to be seated.

The three white men had just finished telling about the

Frontier Hero

stabbing. Whittlesey was white-faced and grim-lipped with pain from his wound.

Chief Wolf rose to his feet and said simply, "Billy bad Indian. But you whipped him. You whipped him enough. He did wrong to stab white trader. But you whip him enough. If white trader die, then you, Owen, kill him. Or I will."

"That's fair enough," Kenton said. "Whittlesey, you don't look like you're going to die. Chief, let your men know that the next time there is an attack like this, they won't get off so easy. I'll see to that myself."

In the middle of the summer word spread that a large band of Indians was gathering near Detroit to attack the frontier. Simon turned his cabin-building over to the other settlers and hurried to Ottoway Town where he met with the Indian chiefs. Black Snake said to him, "We and the white men are brothers now. We were the last to make peace with General Wayne at Greenville; we will also be the last to break it. We are sorry to hear that you have received false news from someone. We are not planning any trouble."

While there was no outright attack by all the Indians, some of their wilder brothers caused much unrest all winter. Kenton continued to raise parties when there were any Indian outrages. In January, One Eye, who had the reputation of being a "bad Indian," went into the Dement cabin where the woman of the house was alone. He demanded food which she refused. He then seized her by the hair and dragged her about until she was unconscious.

"On His Own Hook"

After that he went to the spring house and stole some food.

Kenton was told of the attack that night, and the next morning set out with fifteen men for One Eye's camp. They caught the renegade, tied him up, and each man whipped him a certain number of strokes. That way no one person could be blamed for the punishment. One Eye, however, held Simon responsible. A number of times he was seen near the Kenton cabin and was heard muttering threats that "When the bushes got green he would kill Cutta-ho-tha," the Indians' name for Simon.

Shortly after, while on an errand to the Indians at Stony Creek, Kenton became aware that someone was following him. He whirled around to face One Eye. Simon, like both whites and Indians, had left his gun stacked at the council lodge. But he whipped out his knife and threw it at a distant tree, hitting the trunk dead center with a loud plunk. He strode toward the tree and yanked out his knife, then turned to glare at One Eye. The Indian's face took on a sickly grin as he bobbed his head saying, "Me friend. Me friend."

Kenton had no more trouble with One Eye.

However, another Indian, very intoxicated, came into the cabin one day when Simon was away. He demanded whiskey of Betsey Kenton. She refused. He then grabbed up the year-old Matilda from her crib and ran toward the nearby Indian camp. Betsey ran after him screaming for help. She was met on the way by the tribal chief carrying the baby back to her.

Simon rushed to the camp when he heard about this, ready to deal with the kidnapper. But when the chief

Frontier Hero

promised that the Indians would punish the guilty one, Kenton was satisfied. His own people would make the renegade suffer worse than Simon ever could.

In the hunting camps close to his settlement were old Indian friends. There was Bonah, large, squat and heavy, who had helped capture Simon in 1778. He had claimed him as his own prisoner, guarded him, even whipped him and given him food. He often visited the Kenton cabin, ate at the table with the family, and always asked for gifts.

"Come to think of it, Bonah," Simon said one day, "why should I continue to give you gifts when you were once so mean to me?"

Bonah was silent for a long moment, then he said triumphantly, "Because I didn't kill you!"

John Coon, a white man who had been captured when three years old and reared with the Indians, settled down on Kenton's farm with his squaw and half-breed children.

There were other Indians who made permanent settlement on Kenton's acres. They followed him from place to place as he established new settlements and built new cabins to live in. They had no objection to hunting game for food, but they wanted no part of farming. It was much easier to help themselves from Kenton's brimming corn cribs. Simon's children played with the Indian children and from them picked up the Indian language.

In 1801 Kenton started a school on his land and enrolled the Indian children as well as the white boys and girls of his settlement. One student named Spy Buck was clever at learning, and Kenton took him to Kentucky when he

"On His Own Hook"

returned on a visit, to show off "an Indian who can read and write."

Two years later Kenton's vast holdings in Ohio suddenly vanished. The original landholder there could not meet the payments for his two million acres and Congress canceled the purchase. So Kenton's Ohio possessions were no more.

However, Springfield had been laid out. Betsey Kenton had so named it, "On account of the many and delightful springs within and around the place located for the town."

Simon was not discouraged; on the contrary, he was full of zest for new plans and ventures. In the fall he sent out a friendly Indian, Chi-ux-ko, to hack out Kenton's Trace from Lagonda Creek near Springfield to Newmarket, which lay almost opposite his old Limestone settlement across the Ohio.

Cutting a road through the rank wilderness was slow work, and Kenton labored right along with the party slashing a way through the underbrush. When he reached the river he crossed over with Spy Buck to get supplies. These were needed for the saw and grist mill he was planning to put up on the Lagonda, also for the trading post he would establish.

His saws were brought down from Pittsburgh. His millstones were cut at Laurel Creek in Pennsylvania and hauled twenty-five miles to Redstone Old Fort on the Monongahela. There they were put on a flatboat and sent down the Ohio. From there they were taken by wagon to the millsite one hundred miles distant. These millstones were said to be the best they had ever seen by all the millers who ever used them.

The millstones were on the first wagon that traveled over Kenton's Trace, and it was William Kenton's son Thomas who took it over in May 1802.

Simon, however, did not return to Ohio at the time his grindstones arrived. He was caught up in a tangle of land trouble in Kentucky and then was taken with a serious illness. His wife left their infant daughter, Elizabeth, born December 6, 1801, and went to Washington to nurse him. After a while he recovered, and once he got back home he was afire with his oldtime zest and started building three cabins at once.

His hunger for land was gnawing at his vitals once more. In 1802 he took Felix, a French trader and interpreter, with him and went to visit the Wabash Indians. There, as his son William relates it:

> ... he made an Indian treaty with Tecumseh for nearly all the land between the Miami and the Wabash "on his own hook"—a treaty prohibited by Congress. He was given a treaty signed by Abey Clark, which gave father most of the land between the Miami and the Wabash— near half of Ohio and some of Indiana in return for considerable goods and provisions paid to the Indians and promise to pay more money or goods as long as grass grows and water flows and other stipulations similar to other Indian treaties.

However, Ohio became a state the same year and that instantly made Simon's treaty invalid. The infant govern-

"On His Own Hook"

ment would not allow any one citizen to own "near half of Ohio and some of Indiana" by any private treaty with Tecumseh and his chiefs. Simon hoped to be able to retain at least part of his new holdings, but this wish was not to be granted.

Kenton returned to his home in time for the birth of his daughter Mary, born March 3, 1803.

CHAPTER 11

Trouble in the Settlements

In the spring of 1804 Simon commenced building his mill, but his fine grindstones would lay idle four winters before they were used to grind Ohio corn. He had dozens of things to do and traveled here and there in Ohio and Kentucky on land deals. He was also mixed up in all of the numerous Indian troubles and soon found himself right in the center of the famous Billy George affair. The whites, for lack of any established law and order, of necessity finally took the matter into their own hands.

Billy George was the same notorious "bad Indian" who had caused trouble before. He was a Cherokee who lived with the Shawnee, but his adopted tribe would have little to do with him and Billy lived in a lonely camp at the head of Lagonda Creek. His whipping had taught him a lesson for a while; but now he resumed his habit of visiting the homes of settlers when the husband was away. He would demand food or whiskey, and if these were refused he brandished his tomahawk in a threatening manner.

There had been several mysterious deaths of white men

Trouble in the Settlements

recently, and one night Chi-ux-ko came to Kenton with some news. Billy George had been bragging that he had killed two big white chiefs and now would not be satisfied until he had killed the third and biggest one of all. Chi-ux-ko was sure that Kenton was the "big Chief" that Billy had in mind. He insisted on staying with Simon in order to protect him.

Two nights later Billy George came to Kenton's house and announced that he wanted to sleep there. When it came time to retire, Kenton motioned toward a bed and told Billy to "turn in."

"Not sleepy," Billy said gruffly.

"Then," Simon said, "you'll have to leave our place, or I'll tie you up."

Billy started to draw a knife. Then Chi-ux-ko, who had heard the discussion from another room, came in and Billy slowly pushed his knife back in its sheath. The three men sat up all night before the fire, and the next morning the sullen Billy left.

Simon called together a group of neighboring men to decide what could be done about Billy George.

"None of us will be safe as long as he lives," one of the men said.

His neighbors agreed. There was as yet no government legal agency to handle such a problem, and on the frontier the pioneers had to make and enforce their own laws.

Another man said, "I'm in favor of drawing up a warrant for his arrest. He will be sure to resist being arrested. Then we'll have to shoot him."

Simon fell ill before this rude frontier justice could be

Frontier Hero

administered, but Archibald Dowden, Robert Renick and Jesse Bracken led a small party to Billy's camp. Finding him gone, they cut off meat from a deer he had shot and hung from a tree limb nearby. They cooked it and ate while they waited.

When Billy returned and saw them an angry expression came over his face. As Bracken read the warrant for his arrest he grew further enraged and whipped out his knife. Before he could use his weapon two men shot him dead in his tracks.

The *Western Spy* of October 3, 1804, gave notice of the coming election of a brigadier general, the first election of its kind held since the state of Ohio was formed in 1802.

The following news was printed in that paper in a subsequent issue.

> In October Simon Kenton was duly elected brigadier general of the first division of the Ohio militia—so certified by Major General John S. Gano. This election was held at the court house in Dayton by the commissioned officers of that brigade on the 16th of October.

In 1804 the Louisiana Purchase astonished the world. In 1805 Kenton returned to Missouri, where he and his bride had honeymooned on a long camping trip. Most of his land purchases had fallen through when his Indian treaty had collapsed, and though he still owned much Ohio land, it was in small plots, not the vast empire he had dreamed of.

He took with him to Missouri his son John, now a tall

Trouble in the Settlements

boy of fifteen. They went first to Madrid, where Simon purchased a large plot of land, then on up the Mississippi to St. Charles, whose single street rambled along the river for a mile, lined with small wooden houses. Daniel Boone lived nearby and Simon wanted to visit his old friend.

They came to a clearing in the forest, in the center of which was a neat pioneer cabin. The sound of an axe striking wood rang out a short distance away. A pile of freshly cut logs lay beside the cabin door, and Simon picked up an armload and knocked. Mrs. Boone opened it and gave a cry of delight when she saw who it was.

She cupped her mouth with her hand and shouted, "Daniel, come home. There's a surprise for you here!"

But Daniel did not hurry. The venison was nearly cooked when he came in bearing more wood.

"Whoop la!" he shouted in delight when he saw his old friend. "The sight of you does my old heart good."

Turning to John, he said, "And who is this lad, so straight and strong?"

"I'm John," the boy replied with a grin.

"No! You couldn't be. You were just a small whippersnapper when last I saw you. Now you're taller than me. It makes me feel old to see how you have grown."

Simon was surprised and hurt to see how much Daniel Boone had aged. His hair was silvery white and his face was lined, although his figure was still erect.

When they sat down to eat, Simon asked Boone how things were going.

"Oh, I manage to keep busy," Daniel answered cheerfully. "I trap all the nearby streams and I'm making more money than I ever did farming. The Spaniards gave me a thousand-acre grant. But when the United States made the Louisiana Purchase they canceled my grant. The battle is still being fought in court. I hope to get at least some of it back. So what goes with you, Simon? You don't look much older."

"I am though," Simon said. "Two of my daughters are married. Soon, I expect, I'll be a grandfather."

Kenton stayed for a week, enjoying every minute with the Boones. He told Daniel that when the land gave out in Ohio, he himself might come to Missouri to settle, where there was more "elbow room." John remained behind for an extended visit when his father left for home.

When Simon returned to Ohio he found Indian troubles brewing again. Early in 1806 Tecumseh had gathered his tribe together at the head of Stony Creek, and other tribes were gathered at Wapatomika and Greenville. Kenton received the disturbing word that the Shawnee were preparing for war against the whites. Captain James McPherson came down from his trading post above Urbana to discuss the matter with Simon. Together they decided that the situation was serious enough to send out a warning to the settlers.

McPherson went up one side of the Mad River, Simon up the opposite side, advising the settlers to fort up at the strongest house in their neighborhood.

A group of people gathered at Thomas Kenton's, whose double cabin was better "fortified" than the others around him. There was a well within the enclosure, and juts at the corners had portholes from which to shoot. Simon and

Trouble in the Settlements

his family stayed there the first night, but decided the next morning to go to Joseph Reynold's settlement. A great number of people had already gathered at that place because there were many more strong cabins.

Continual rain poured down, but sentinels kept watch day and night. The settlers were grateful that there was no attack, yet they were growing weary of the long-drawn-out suspense. Simon asked Captain McPherson and Charles McIlvane to go with him to parley with the Indians. They arrived at the main village in the afternoon and were about to head toward the council lodge when an Indian rushed up to them. He told them that they were not to enter the council but that the Shawnee would meet them afterward at another lodge.

Toward evening eighteen Indians daubed with war paint and wearing painted feathers came in and sat cross-legged in a circle.

Simon rose and said, "We, your friends, believe that we have much reason to be alarmed by the information we get from our white friends and your neighbors. We, your brothers, wish for nothing but true friendship."

He handed the chief a strip of white wampum.

The chief took the gift and said, "We intend no harm. We thank the Great Spirit that we are still brothers and wish that true friendship will exist between us."

After further talk, when Simon and his party left, the Indians all extended their left hands in a cool manner. In spite of this aloof attitude, the settlers felt that something had been accomplished and that danger was over for the time being.

Frontier Hero

An English traveler, Thomas Ashe, who visited the settlement on Mad River in 1806, wrote a colorful description of the pioneer settlement:

> I visited at least one hundred farms and found the inhabitants in the possession of abundance of every common necessary and even absolute comfort essential to a modest and unassuming life. You who have always been accustomed to the refinements of luxury will scarcely be able to conceive how these settlers, with no other clothing than coarse homemade apparel, with no other shelter but a log house constructed with the rudest art, and with no food but of the coarsest kind and destitute of coffee, tea, wine and foreign spirits can enjoy any happiness; and yet as I observe, to judge from their manners, language and external application, their state may be envied by all wealthy and most refined natures. They are composed of all nations and live as yet in a kind of native freedom and independence; in a kind of equality of rank which banishes all distinctions but those of age and merit, for the old control the parochial administration, and the learned govern the legal and those affairs pertaining to worship. However, as population increases, and as towns and villages abound, vice, which appears in the propensity of man, will erect its power and call for the influence of the general regulation of the State and destroy the innocent and primitive characters which now distinguish the republic of the Mad River. Nothing in truth can be more primitive. Justice is administered with decency, but no forms. In the open air and on Sunday the people gather together in appointed groves and silently attend to any person endowed with the grace and talent of instruction.

Trouble in the Settlements

Thomas Ashe also enjoyed samples of frontier sociability, such as when all of the neighbors gathered to help a friend erect a cabin or took part in a corn-husking bee. He decided that the pioneers were happier than people who lived in centers of civilization.

While Kenton was away on one of his many mysterious trips, a son, William Miller, was born. Simon returned, bringing a bundle of pear trees, and when he heard this news he planted a row of them behind his house to mark the event.

He found that new neighbors, the McBeths, had settled on a farm three miles to the north and rode over to call on them. Simon approved the sturdy cabin they had built with portholes and an iron-strapped door. The population of Mad River had doubled within the year, making the settlement better equipped to meet the Indian trouble which would rise again in the spring. Then a report came from Fort Wayne that the redskins were gathering at Greenville, as they had the year before. Some eight hundred warriors were there, including Tecumseh's brother, called the Prophet, whose influence was powerful.

Simon considered the situation serious enough to justify a dangerous trip into the Indian camp, and with him went James McPherson, James Reed and William Ward. The little group succeeded in arranging for a council between the Indians and the white men in the Mad Valley. They met at McPherson's home, but the natives were in such a sullen mood that the meeting was quickly changed to an open space near Kenton's mill at Lagonda. On the way to the mill they went "armed to the teeth, two and two

Frontier Hero

abreast, an Indian and a white man together throughout the whole line of march."

As they reached McBeth's cabin halfway on their journey, the Indians were told to leave their tomahawks at Major Moore's gun shop across the road. But all of the men, Indian and white, retained their guns. It had been agreed that at the council grounds, all armed men not taking part in the parley should stand at the rear, each on his own side. The chiefs and the principal white men would not carry arms, but advance empty-handed to the center of the circle.

Tecumseh, however, stalked with contempt to the center of the council, boldly carrying his pipe tomahawk. When told that everyone else in the council had given up his tomahawk, he grumbled that he wished to smoke. Thereupon one of the white men handed him a corncob pipe. Tecumseh frowned at the man and tossed the gift over his shoulder, but grudgingly handed his tomahawk to one of his men who carried it to the rear of the Indian party.

It was Kenton, Whiteman, McPherson and Ward who were the spokesmen for the whites. The record which has come down to us concerning the important meeting states that the others were very excited in speech and manner, but that Kenton, who had dealt with the Indians for thirty-six years, was calm and in command of himself. When it came his turn to speak, his manner and words carried far more weight than those of the others.

Simon Kenton was always described as a man of few words; but when he spoke his words were impressive. He

Trouble in the Settlements

had attended so many councils with the Indians that he knew their rituals and the right things to say. As always, he was a man without fear, and he bore himself as if he knew that his life was a charmed one. He behaved with the stolidity and dignity of an Indian.

Tecumseh and his tribesmen listened to him with respect. After many speeches on both sides an understanding was reached and Indian trouble was averted.

CHAPTER 12

Simon's Last War

For the next two years Kenton occupied himself with his mill and store on the Lagonda. Then he took one of his mysterious trips, leaving his business in charge of a clerk named James Robinson. He had great confidence in the man, but unfortunately for Simon, Robinson proved to be a thief. He collected all of the cash he could get from outstanding accounts owed to Kenton and left the country with the money. No trace of him could be found.

With the ending of the Indian wars, immigration to Kentucky and Ohio pushed forward in a constant stream. Land had become more valuable, but there had been great irregularity in the first entries and surveys. Although Simon was at one time very rich in land, one claim after another failed to meet legal requirements and he was enmeshed in a maze of lawsuits. Being completely unlettered and unacquainted with legal proceedings, every advantage was taken of his ignorance. In a few years the technicalities and uncertainties of the law stripped Simon Kenton of the earnings he had bought with his great services. The same judicial procedures sent him into the evening of his life penniless and dejected, to spend his few remaining years in poverty and want.

On his return to Lagonda, after Robinson's vicious theft of his money and goods, Simon began to restock his store. Much of his merchandise came from Kentucky over Kenton's Trace. As usual, the better he was supplied with stock, the more he gave credit to everyone who asked for it. Here, as at Washington, some men made a living by trading at Kenton's store without paying for the goods. As a result his earnings were very meager.

The wanderlust hit him again and he traveled up to St. Charles to visit Daniel Boone once more and get his son John whom he had left there. While at Boone's he learned that his old friends, John Edgar the storekeeper and his wife, who had been kind to him during his captivity in Detroit, were living at Kaskaskia. He and John decided to travel a full day's journey away from their route to visit the Edgars.

On their way Simon said, "It was through this very land that I guided General George Rogers Clark. There is a great man I should like to have you know. He was as strong and fiery as lightning. This country was all wilderness then. Now look at it. Once rude cabins clustered here. Now look at the fine houses."

The Edgars lived in one of the most imposing residences and were delighted to receive Simon and John as their guests. There were good food and a flood of reminiscenses which brought back vivid memories. Simon retold the multitude of dangers through which he had passed.

"Every time I escaped death," he said, "I had a feeling of destiny—as though I was being spared for a purpose. I reckon it was to protect the settlers and to help build up the frontier."

"You have served that purpose well." John Edgar nodded.

It was while he was visiting his old friends that the idea was born for his next business venture—his Missouri stores. John Edgar knew a great deal about storekeeping and his enthusiasm helped to kindle that of Kenton.

"Listen, John," Simon ordered. "I'm sending you back here next year with stocks of goods. We will open two stores, one here at St. Charles and another at St. Louis."

"You'll do well in those places," Edgar told him.

The following year Kenton did as he had promised. He sent his son John and William McCarty, one of his sons-in-law, to open the two stores. They drove covered wagons carrying $18,000 worth of supplies—all of the things that were needed for trade in those days: corn, flour, tobacco, moccasins, leggings, knives, ammunition, blankets, bolts of cloth, guns, paints, black and white wampum and many other things.

Simon had sold some of his Kentucky lands for $36,000. Then he turned right around and bought a "Spanish grant," paying $16,000 down and promising to pay $8000 more. This amount he planned to pay out of the profits of the two stores. But John and McCarty mismanaged both places; there were no profits.

Simon's Last War

Simon had never professed to be a religious man, although he had attended church services regularly. But when he returned from his last trip he attended a camp meeting and became converted. His friends stated that he did not appear too much changed by his conversion. It was said of him:

> He was always greatly beloved; he always played with children and they liked him; his manner, especially to women and children was courteous and tender; the expression of his face was mild; his voice low and gentle. There was never a taint of wrong-doing attached to him. His habits were natural; he did not indulge in even the temperate use of liquors; he used tobacco only in snuff; he was abstemious all of his life—simple and unsophisticated in everyday life; for a man without scholastic culture he was remarkable chaste in behavior and conversation.

Simon was unable to pay the $8000 he had promised on his Spanish grant, so he lost not only the land but the large down payment he had made on it. For nearly a year he had been living in the shadow of imprisonment on the old debtor's law. A Kentucky man to whom he owed money sent lawyers into Ohio to recover a debt which Simon claimed was unjust. He refused to pay it, and the debtor's law was invoked.

Under that old law his body could be seized and held until the debt was paid, so it was decreed that he must go to jail. The Champaign County jail was in Urbana. The county was settled largely by his "Boys," men who had defended the frontier with Kenton, his blood relatives and scores of in-laws. These people quickly elected Simon to be his own jailer. One of the first records of the county stated: "Found Philip Jarboe and have his body in court; found Simon Kenton, but he refuses to be arrested."

He took his time about closing up his dwindling affairs in Springfield and Lagonda. His mill and store had gone to ruin financially, as had his two stores in St. Charles and St. Louis. His farm in Springfield had never been properly cleared and he also lost it.

When he got around to the burdensome task of serving out his prison term he took his family and went to Urbana. There Kenton took his oath of office as jailer, and they lived in the county jail building where they had five rooms upstairs and one below. Here he stayed for two years to fulfill his sentence. And here one of his daughters was born, another died, and two were married.

Being "imprisoned" for debt did not mean that he must be confined to a cell. Three friends signed his bond which allowed him to move from one end of the town to the other; but the edge of town on either end was as far as he could go. His white-headed figure became a familiar sight on the village street. Since his rifle-carrying days were over he always carried a staff, grasped firmly about a foot from the top. This end was badly charred for he used it not only as a cane but as a poker to stir up the fire. He would always walk to the edge of the town as though he were going to step beyond the boundary, then bring himself to a stop and give a quick turn with military precision.

When his little daughter Elizabeth died, he attended the

Simon's Last War

services in the family room on the lower story. Then he accompanied the small coffin to the edge of town, stopped quickly at the boundary and turned with misty eyes to stalk back to the jail.

Simon had kept what was left of the supplies from his store at Lagonda in a shed behind the jail. The Indians came to Urbana bringing bear, deer, and wolf skins, moccasins, leggings, maple sugar and honey. Thus he was able to trade with them and managed to live comfortably.

Kenton was freed in 1811 and quickly built a cabin in Urbana for his family. Then he made a trip to Missouri to check on his ill-fated business ventures. There was nothing left of his St. Louis project. John had sold it out and with the proceeds had bought one hundred traps for a fur-trading expedition up the Missouri. He was caught by Indians who stole all of his traps and nearly took his life.

John sent a contrite letter home vowing that he would not return until he could repay every penny that he had lost. Simon never saw his son again. Years later he learned that the boy had gone to Mexico, joined a revolutionary party and been killed.

Things were just as bad at St. Charles. As usual Simon had been too trusting. The stock had been squandered and his entire $18,000 was lost.

Nature also turned on Kenton. Beginning in December 1811 an earthquake continued for five months to send out tremors felt from New Orleans to Detroit and from South Carolina to southern California. "The Mississippi ran backward" and tore out new banks for itself. It washed

Frontier Hero

away hundreds of acres of rich lands, including most of Simon Kenton's purchases.

Then came the War of 1812, the struggle between Great Britain and her former colonies. It came about because England impressed American seamen into her navy to serve in Britain's war against Napoleon and France, and because the English blockaded United States waters. Such highhanded tactics could not be tolerated, and for the second time America went to war against her mother country.

In September the first of the Kentucky troops passed through Urbana to join General Harrison on the frontier. From that time on, as one of his friends wrote—

> Kenton's home was an inn where the guests did not pay. His house was a home to the sick and the afflicted. He visited the camps and if any needed assistance he gave it without accepting payment. His family were almost like servants from the time Hull came through until peace was made. One stormy evening and a deep snow on the ground, he was up in town where he saw a company of packhorsemen that could not get shelter. There was one of them sick and he took them all to his house.

His Urbana home has been described as

> ... a log house of the most primitive style, with a dirt floor and a stump left standing in the center, which, properly dug out, formed the then necessary equipment of a hominy mortar. This was the family room of a double cabin, the other being ten feet behind it and divided into sleeping chambers with sleeping lofts above. It can be

Simon's Last War

imagined what these cabins were like when to Kenton's large family were added old friends, sick soldiers, and packhorsemen from Kentucky to be bedded and fed.

Kenton was once again called upon to raise and lead a punitive expedition against the Indians. He was to pursue a band of "British Indians" who had murdered the Thomas family near Solomon's Town. The thirty men under his command followed the trail along the Miami River, over open spots alternating with dense brush. It was dangerous country, for the redskins might be hiding in any of the thickets through which they pushed.

Three natives from Lewiston, a supposedly friendly Indian camp, came up and offered to guide the Kenton party to the enemy. Simon put the "guides" in front and kept them in sight. Coming to a high bluff the guides let out three war whoops; as he had suspected, they were spies.

He halted his party and told them to train their rifles on the opposite shore while he and several of his men crossed the river and scouted. Coming back he said, "We have been pursuing hostile Indians all day. And our guides have been leading us straight into an ambush. I advise a quick retreat."

There were many who wanted to press on, some even accusing him of being afraid.

Simon spoke quietly, "It is not my life, which is now well nigh spent, that I am trying to save; it is your own. And let those who do not believe me take up the line of march and pursue the enemy beyond the hearing of the war whoops, and they will never return. You have only

Frontier Hero

to cross to the other side of the stream to see the enemy camp."

Kenton's advice was heeded and the party returned unharmed from the scout.

It was impossible for the old war horse to remain at home when there was another war going on. When Governor Shelby came through Urbana with hundreds of Kenton's old friends among his troops, Kenton joined them. Shelby welcomed him as a counselor and adviser. But when his family heard of his plans they protested loudly. He was fifty-eight years old and still limped a bit from the leg he had broken a year ago. His wife and children told him that he could not stand the rigors of a long campaign.

Simon pretended to agree and smiled when his family sighed with relief as Shelby marched off. A short time later he saddled his horse and rode away, sending word back by a neighbor that he was on his way to join Shelby.

Kenton was with the army in Canada and was there when the great chief Tecumseh was reported to be killed. He was sent for to identify the body.

"That," Simon stated flatly, "is not Tecumseh! I have seen him too often—knew him too well. This is not the chief. The Indians have too much respect for their dead ever to leave Tecumseh behind. This is some other man."

In that campaign Kenton thought the British showed themselves to be poor fighters. He was permitted to move freely among the American troops, a privileged member of Shelby's army. Then with the last days of this campaign Kenton's marvelous fighting career came to an end.

Simon's Last War

In 1813, England sued for peace with the United States. Commissioners from the two countries met at Ghent, Belgium. The treaty provided for restoration of all land captured by either side, leaving ownership as it was before the war. The peace commission was appointed to decide the boundary between Canada and the United States. There was no reference to the chief cause of the war—the impressment of American seamen—but the question never again troubled the two countries.

For forty-two years Kenton had lived on the frontier and had defended it at the risk of his own life time after time. Now the frontier borders lay to the west. The British had been driven north beyond the Great Lakes, and the Indians were retreating steadily westward across the Mississippi. Civilization was sweeping west after them, changing forests to fields. Simon's work in blazing and defending the long trail was finished. It had taken all of his youth and all of his middle years. Now he stood at the edge of old age, but his back was still straight and his eyes still keen.

CHAPTER 13

Kentucky Returns a Favor

Colonel William Ward was in the Dunmore War with Kenton, and the two men became firm friends. Later on Ward built a home on the farm next to Simon's, and they went on numerous Indian missions together. Ward was a southern gentleman from Virginia, tall and distinguished-looking, with broad shoulders, high cheekbones and penetrating eyes. He was always dressed in fine clothes at the height of fashion, while Kenton in contrast always wore the garb of a frontiersman. Yet for almost a quarter of a century the two men not only were the best of friends but became partners in land deals.

Before Kenton had moved to Ohio he and Ward were constant companions on trips across the river to look for land. Simon was wise about the values of land and shrewd in land trades, but he had too much faith in human nature. Once a paper was signed and some money paid, to Simon the matter was finished. His ignorance and carelessness about law and taxes were colossal. He himself would not think of taking advantage of lapsed payments to foreclose

Kentucky Returns A Favor

on the land of another man, and he failed to take into account the fact that others were not so charitable.

Of the hundreds of thousands of dollars and the hundreds of thousands of acres of land that had passed through Kenton's hands, very few of either were left by 1832. His brother John had mismanaged the property left in his care. His Missouri lands had gone by flood following the earthquake and by default. Most of his Ohio land went because he could not meet the payments. But for many years he thought himself still rich in lands held in partnership with Colonel Ward.

In 1818, however, Kenton discovered that he was not rich in land or anything else. Simon brought suit against his old friend for what he thought was his share of some properties in Champaign County.

As is stated in the *History of Champaign County:*

> It is claimed that Ward furnished some capital and his knowledge of land titles and conveyances. Kenton was familiar with the country and knew of choice locations. To the latter was entrusted the payment of taxes, which Ward claims he neglected, involving loss to him, and that he closed his partnership with Kenton by written articles. The consequence was that Ward was accused of cheating Kenton, but there is no evidence to confirm the charge, and on the other hand, Kenton, well-meaning, honest and upright, was nevertheless known to be careless and shiftless in business matters. . . .

Whatever the real facts are, it is true that Simon became poorer and poorer while Ward became richer and richer.

Frontier Hero

Gone forever were the good old days. Gone was the brick, two-storied house and the acres of fertile land farmed by tenants. Gone were the slaves and the brimming corn cribs and an easy way of life. Gone were the trading stores on which Simon and his friends could draw without limit and without accounting. His first child was born to riches. His last was born to poverty.

Simon's excessive generosity often irked the members of his family. He insisted rightly that his children get as much schooling as the frontier offered; but he also spent considerable money helping to educate young men of exceptional ability.

When he was living in Urbana one of his neighbors wrote, "Simon was always hard-pressed to make ends meet."

At one time when he was about to return to Kentucky on one of his many business trips, he was forced to appeal to a neighbor, Zephaniah Luce.

"Zeph," he said, greatly embarrassed, "would you help out while I am gone by supplying my family with any food they may need? I'll pay you back when I return."

"I know you will," Luce replied. "I'll be glad to furnish anything your wife and children may need. You've always been so generous in helping others that they in turn should be willing to help you out."

True to his promise, Simon paid Zephaniah soon after his return. Kenton's carelessness in business dealings seems to have centered only in his tangled land operations. There is no indication that he failed to meet his daily obligations to his friends and neighbors.

Kentucky Returns A Favor

As he grew poorer he became desperate and frequently went off on land-trading trips. He would sell lands by quitclaim deeds and take in exchange whatever he could get—horses, cattle, wagons or cloth. These he would bring back to Urbana by wagon, where he would trade the merchandise to his neighbors for food, or whatever his family needed. Simon junior was now a young man who did the farming and raising of cattle.

In 1818 Simon received news that his good friend George Rogers Clark had died.

Simon shook his head in sorrow, then said: "It's too bad that no one ever wrote a book about General Clark." Nodding, he added, "And for that matter someone should have written one about Dan Boone. He's getting along in years and won't live much longer."

"Why shouldn't you have a book written about you?" Elizabeth spoke up. "You're as great as they are. The part you played in protecting the frontier was as great. I wish I had enough education and had the time. I'd write it myself. But I'm saving my notes on your adventures. Someday a writer will come by and want to do a book about you."

The passing of Clark was the first historic break with old times in Kenton's life, and it brought to the surface of his mind many memories. These he told to Elizabeth and her quill pen hurried across the pages as she wrote down his reminiscences.

After Simon junior married and went to live on a place of his own, Kenton had no one to run his farm for him.

Frontier Hero

William was still but a boy, and the eldest daughter Nancy had died the previous winter.

The brick house at Washington which had been sold so long ago had never actually been paid for, and Simon took in place of money a sixteen-hundred-acre tract of land on the Mad River about three miles north of Zanesfield. Kenton had been so unlucky with land taken in his own name that he deeded this tract to young Simon, in trust for the seven children still living. It was evenly divided among them, to be deeded to them by Simon junior as soon as they came of age. But despite his precautions that land, too, went little by little to pay old debts. Only one share was left, held by his daughter Matilda, and on it one day a small cabin would be built for Simon and Elizabeth to spend their last days.

At about that earlier time, however, he bought sixty-five acres near Zanesfield for himself. Here within sight of the place where he had run his first gantlet, Simon moved in 1820 with his wife and the four children still living at home: Mary, William, Elizabeth and Ruth Jane. His dreams of an empire had long since faded. Now he was satisfied with sixty-five acres, he who had once owned a three-thousand-acre tract on Machachack Prairie. The family lived in a partly finished cabin on the new tract while Simon finished a house in the center of a large cleared space. Nearby was a fine sugar camp of several hundred maple trees, and on one side was an apple orchard grown from seeds planted by the Shawnee. This was the site of the Indian village where Simon Girty had rescued him.

Kentucky Returns A Favor

Later in 1820 Simon was sent for to testify in a land case. It was a trick. No sooner had he reached Kentucky than he was seized and imprisoned in the Mason County jail for a debt.

Kenton protested furiously. The "debt" under which he was held involved a gift he had made to an old friend, McConnell. The friend had settled there and reared his family. Before his death he advised the children to let the place go, as it was a gift, not a purchase, from Kenton. However, after McConnell's death, his children pressed the claim through one of the sons whom Simon had educated as a lawyer.

A number of Kenton's friends offered to pay the "debt" but Simon refused. He would not pay it himself or allow any of his friends to pay the unjust claim. They did insist upon paying his security that he would keep his bounds, which at first comprised ten acres. Later these were extended to the town limits and then to the county boundaries. Simon had to report to his jailer each night and was supposed to sleep in the debtor's cell and eat at the jailer's table. But he often slept out and ate where he pleased. It was not strange that his jailer was so lenient. He was Thomas Williams, the man with whom Simon had come down the Ohio in 1775 and landed at Limestone where the cane lands began, and with whom he took "planting possession" in Mason County.

It was while in jail that he heard of Daniel Boone's death in Missouri. First Clark and now Boone. Simon now began to wonder when his own time would come.

His wife made several horseback trips during the year

Frontier Hero

to visit him, bringing William with her. On one of those trips she left the boy to live with his uncle John, Simon's brother. William would be company for his father and go to school with the children of his father's old friends.

At this time John Bickley and Thomas Pickett came to talk with Kenton about writing his biography, asking and getting permission to use Elizabeth's notes. They took voluminous notes and put out a prospectus for subscribers who were to pay one dollar a copy for the book. But signers were few and the book remained unwritten. In 1832 the material would appear in *Sketches of Western Adventure* by John Alexander McClung; then in 1835 as a biographical sketch by John McDonald in the *Western Christian Advocate*.

As the months passed, Kenton's friends grew increasingly angry over his imprisonment. One of them, William Worthington, was re-elected a member of the Kentucky Legislature from Mason County on the ground of repealing the hated debtor's law.

Now that he was no longer in legal jeopardy Simon remained in Kentucky for two years, trying to save what little land he still owned. He had no more "fine lands," and all that was left were little tracts of mountain wastes on which he could scarcely pay the taxes. The next spring he fell ill and stayed at his brother John's house, where for nearly two weeks he thought he was about to die. His wife came from Ohio on horseback to care for him.

When he was better his wife and William returned to Ohio but Simon remained in Kentucky for a few months to recover his strength. His illness depressed him and he

Kentucky Returns A Favor

felt that he was outliving his era. He said to friends, "When I first saw this region those tall yellow poplars were mere saplings. Now look at them—many of them two feet through and some dying. And here I am yet."

Finally Kenton returned to his home in Ohio only to be promptly put in the Urbana jail, for the old debtor's law still held in that state. The same claimants who had forced his imprisonment in Kentucky were responsible. Probably Kenton would have stayed in jail for the rest of his life before he paid the unjust claim, but lawyer Henry Bacon cleared Simon of the charge.

In 1824 he was called back to Kentucky as witness in an important land suit. In court at Washington on June 25, 1824, he talked freely of "war roads," "buffalo traces" and the famous "powder route" followed in 1777.

A man who met him at the time speaks of Kenton at sixty-nine as a "stout athletic man—perhaps a child of nature—in possession of the vigorous organism mentally and physically."

Court orders continued to pester Kenton. One day David Smith, an Urbana constable, followed him into a friend's house.

"Father Kenton," he said, "among all the things I ever had to do this hurts my feelings the most."

He then thrust out a summons to appear before Squire Markley to answer to a suit brought by the Urbana jailer for food and lodging furnished Simon while he was in jail two years ago.

"Ho!" snorted Simon. "I paid what I thought was enough before I left. More would be too much."

Frontier Hero

John Parkison, his son-in-law, and his nephew, John Arrowsmith, went his bail.

When the case came to trial the squire asked the jailer, "Did General Kenton go voluntarily to you and seek board and lodging?"

"No," replied the jailer. "He was brought there by others and jailed."

"Then," said the squire, "you must have recourse to those who brought him there." The squire then dismissed Kenton's case.

There were times, however, when he did not reach court, for friends gladly helped him to avoid service. Major James Galloway needed Simon's testimony in reference to a land case of his own. Kenton said he was reluctant to appear in court for fear papers would be served on him that might keep him in debtor's jail. Galloway then suggested that they ride to Kentucky where Simon's deposition could be taken and used instead of his direct testimony. They took the trail to Sandusky—the area of his old gantlet runs and his hopeless march as a captive of the Indians forty-eight years ago.

Eighty thousand acres of mountain land—the last of Kenton's holdings—was gone. They had been sold by the state for taxes and the state bid them in. It was late fall of 1826 when Simon at last made up his mind to request a favor of the state of Kentucky—to ask her to give those mountain wastes back to him. None of these acres were in his original holdings. He had been too wise to make locations of his own on such worthless land, but he had taken the tracts for bad debts. A great-nephew,

Kentucky Returns A Favor

Mason Arrowsmith, went with him. Simon considered the trip a sort of vacation and visited relatives and friends along the way.

One of his first visits was to General Whiteman, near Clifton, Ohio. Simon found his comrade of the Kenton Station days sick in bed from the effects of old exposures in early Indian warfare.

"I'm sorry to find you laid up," Kenton said.

General Whiteman smiled ruefully. "I'm sorry myself. If I had anticipated this, I probably never would have exposed my life and health for an ungrateful country. With my present knowledge of human nature and the world, I believe I would not under similar circumstances do it over again."

Kenton was sitting before the fire with his hands on his long staff. For a long moment he rested his head on his hands, pondering the matter.

Suddenly he raised his head and said emphatically, "Ben, I have known you from the time you were a boy. I thought I knew you better than either of my own sons, but if these are the honest expressions of your feelings, I never knew you." He paused, then went on with an affectionate twinkle in his eyes, "but I can't help believing that if the test came and you were young again, you would be as ready as ever to shoulder your rifle and serve your country."

The general sighed. "You're a wise one, Simon," his old friend admitted. "I suppose you are right. I would do that very thing and so would you."

When Kenton reached Frankfort, Kentucky, he sought

Frontier Hero

out the senator from Mason County, James Ward. He asked Ward to petition the legislature for the return of his lands in the mountains, which had been taken for nonpayment of taxes.

"I'll be glad to do all that I can to help you," Senator Ward assured him. "Your services to the state have been great. You deserve this favor and much more. It's a crime that you were so long and unjustly imprisoned."

Another friend had met Kenton, and upon learning his errand bought him a good new suit so that he could appear before the legislature in style.

His case was reported January 4, 1827, and passed the Senate with little opposition twelve days later. It passed the House on the twenty-third by a vote of sixty-seven to seventeen. At the end of the session a large reception was held in Kenton's honor and everyone shook his hand; then he was seated in the speaker's chair.

CHAPTER 14

End of the Trail

Following the release of his Kentucky lands a concerted movement was started in both Ohio and Kentucky to get a pension for Simon Kenton. But it would take a long time to accomplish this purpose.

In spite of the fact that he was beginning to show his age he still kept up his trips between Ohio and Kentucky, without, however, increasing his fortunes.

His brother John had died in April, 1827, and Kenton went to see if there was anything left of the property he had given to John in trust. What few records existed were so mixed up that Simon was unable to tell what had become of the lands. All that he was able to discover was that there was nothing left.

From now on he would be visited by biographers who planned to write his history while he was still alive. They considered it important to take down notes from a man who had seen the unfolding panorama of midwestern history and who had played such an active part in making it.

At last the "act for the relief of General Simon Kenton"

was approved and signed by his old friend of Revolutionary days—President Andrew Jackson. Kenton would receive a pension for the rest of his life of twenty dollars a month. At that time he could live comfortably on this amount.

In 1830 Simon gave over the handling of his affairs to his son William, who was now grown up.

So began a life of leisure for the old pioneer. On Sundays he and his wife attended the little church at Zanesfield. He would walk ahead and his wife follow behind him a few steps, as was the custom of old people of that day.

On the weekdays when the mill was working he would ride down the road on his horse with a sack of corn behind the saddle. Then he would take home the ground cornmeal. Other days he would walk or ride his pony to visit the neighbors. Always he greeted the housewife with these words, "You know I like hominy. Have you got any hominy?"

If the reply was "Yes," Simon would say with a grin, "Well, then I'll stay and visit with you."

He would sit before the fireplace in winter prodding the fire with his long staff. In summer he would sit under the trees, sometimes dozing, sometimes simply sitting in thoughtful silence for hours on end. The chores of any household went on around him as though he were a member of the family.

Life was ebbing and flowing about him. Now it was William who was talking about getting married. Simon gave him the Zanesfield cabin as a wedding gift and moved

End of the Trail

four miles north. There a new two-room cabin had been built for him and Elizabeth in his daughter Matilda's side yard. This would be his last cabin; but he still talked of "going West."

He was looking forward now to the Fifty Year Meeting that he and his comrades had planned with George Rogers Clark years before. The date was drawing near and letters were being exchanged by the survivors of Clark's Campaign of 1782. Writers of the letters congratulated each other for "lasting this long."

In June, Simon had his wife write his letters and send them out to summon the survivors, but no more than twenty could be found in Kentucky. In Ohio he could find only himself and James Galloway. Finally he addressed his invitation to "The Citizens of the Western Country" and the reunion was extended to take in everyone who had aided in the conquest of the West.

The celebration was to be held on the fourth of November in Cincinnati, site of Old Fort Washington. They were to meet on the Sabbath, the day before, so they could attend church service together. Then on Monday the old friends would gather on the grounds of the fort to "take final adieu, to meet no more until we all shall meet in a world of spirits." Throughout the whole United States the innkeepers, captains of steamboats and owners of stages were urged to make generous provision for the journeys of "their old fathers of the West."

In July, Parson James Crow came to Simon's cabin from Zanesfield with a letter he had received from Kentucky. An important land suit was to be settled there and

Frontier Hero

Kenton's deposition and presence were absolutely necessary to find a corner in order to establish the claim. He would be paid fifty dollars and expenses both ways.

So in the early fall Simon and his wife set out for their last visit to Kentucky. He was dressed in his very best suit, the one worn when he appeared to petition the legislature for the release of his lands. He also wore his broad-brimmed hat. His wife wore her best also, a brown cassimere with polk dots and a green satin bonnet.

Now it was no longer necessary to take the long trip over Kenton's Trace on horseback. They rode in style by carriage to Dayton, then by stage to Cincinnati, and from there by steamboat to old Limestone and Washington.

Memories more than fifty years old rose in Kenton's mind when he made his deposition at Washington. It aroused his recollections of George Rogers Clark to such an extent that he talked about his hero at great length, and his wife wrote down what he said.

When he went out to establish the land for the child of his old comrade John Todd, many men were present to witness the identification of the corner.

"Right over there," Simon said, pointing, "was where we held an encampment. There is the very tree which I shot at as a mark."

He pulled out his pocket knife and jabbed at the tree until he found the lead bullet he had fired years ago. Simon Kenton triumphantly proved the corner.

It was while he was in Kentucky that he was shown a new book, McClung's *Sketches of Western Adventure*, which contained a brief biography of Simon Kenton. He

End of the Trail

was not greatly impressed by the sketch, for he thought it was too brief.

Kenton's wife, Elizabeth, was kept busy taking care of the correspondence made necessary for the Fifty Year Meeting. Newport and Covington were making elaborate preparations to entertain the pioneers, but Cincinnati would be the main stopping place. Old Fort Washington was where Clark's two blockhouses had been built in 1782, and these were the nucleus of the city on the hill. But of Clark's fourteen hundred fighters, only fifteen were coming to the reunion. Death had claimed most of them; others were too feeble to make the journey.

Then came an enemy which neither the pioneers nor anyone else could conquer—Asiatic cholera. Simon and his wife were already on the way and reached Cincinnati. But news of the epidemic spread like wildfire and most of the pioneers were stopped on their way or before they got started. There would be no Fifty Year Meeting. Citizens had fled the city leaving only the sick and the dying and those who would take care of them. The Kentons stayed overnight with a friend, then left the nearly deserted city. Before their departure Simon saw a coffin being handed through a window across the street. This was another cholera victim.

Kenton was keenly disappointed but resigned as they took the stage from Cincinnati to Xenia. "Hm!" Simon said as they rode on the swaying vehicle. "How's this for luxury, Betsey? It sure does beat riding horseback, doesn't it?"

"It certainly does," Betsey replied.

Frontier Hero

Relatives met them at Xenia and took them by carriage to Chillicothe Old Town and Kenton reminisced about this place. It had been the scene fifty-four years ago of his recovering horses from the Indians and of his wild ride when he was tied flat on the back of a wild stallion. It was also the scene of his first gantlet race. At Chillicothe a big reception was held for him, and he was asked to take a party over the old ground and retell his stirring adventures.

The Kenton relatives took the old couple to Springfield where they were met by other kin, then put into a stage to continue their journey alone.

Kenton was sad that the Fifty Year Meeting had ended in failure. He had looked forward so long to seeing his old pioneer friends; it would have been a fitting climax to his life. There was a chill in the air on the day he returned, and his son-in-law came over to build up a fire. Simon sat before it, with his staff close at hand. He sighed as he sank back into his favorite chair. There would be no more trips for him, except to visit the neighbors. There would be no more adventures.

Simon and Elizabeth attended their last camp meeting that year—a large meeting from several counties where he saw many of his old friends.

Several Indian preachers were at the camp meeting, and Kenton was placed among them on the platform. One of them arose and told the story of the Crucifixion with pantomime so expressively that the audience was moved and awed. Then he spoke of peace on earth—of himself and

End of the Trail

Kenton once enemies, now friends seated beside each other.

William and his wife left that year for Indiana. The lure of new country had the same appeal for the son as it had for his father.

Kenton's eyes misted over when he said good-by. "I'll be going west again myself one of these days," he said. But in his heart he knew that his traveling days were over.

Judith, Kenton's granddaughter, came over from her parents' house not a hundred yards away, so that they would not be alone, and lived with them, helping Elizabeth with the work.

By 1835 Simon's mind had begun to fail considerably. He still liked to talk about old times, but he would get several incidents mixed together and become excited over his failure to remember well. Yet, when he was not disturbed by trying to remember scenes from the past he was a serene old man. He met with gracious dignity the occasional visitors or travelers who stopped by especially to meet the famous old pioneer.

He still liked to move slowly along the paths which led to nearby neighbors, and as he walked with his long staff he still studied the trail for "sign." He watched the lay of the land as intently as he had in the days when hostile Indians might be lurking behind any bush.

Finally he became so feeble that he had to give up his walks and sit all day by his fire.

A month before his death, Sunday meeting was held in his daughter Matilda's home, and two men carried Simon across the yard and into the house. Service was held inside

Frontier Hero

for the neighborhood. Simon tried hard to keep awake but his head bobbed on his chest from time to time.

The sands of time were running faster for him now. He never was ill; he simply "ran down." One day he did not arise from his bed. When Elizabeth brought him his breakfast he said to her," I have fought my last battle, and this one is the hardest of all."

"Oh, no, Simon, you must not talk that way," she cried, an expression of alarm on her face.

"You must not grieve for me, Betsey." His soft voice had become weaker. "Mine has been a good life. I spent the best of my years and energies in saving the frontier from barbarism. Now my work is done...."

It was April 29, 1836. All day he lay dozing while Elizabeth hovered over him. Friends and relatives who heard he was dying came in to see him. He recognized them and spoke to them briefly. Then, in the evening he gave a great sigh and turned his face to the wall. It was "like a candle going out." A great life was ended.

Simon had not wished a military funeral, so it was a simple ceremony attended only by close relatives and neighbors. He had long ago picked out the site for his grave—at the foot of the little hill where his cabin had stood on the Sandusky Road.

Four years after his death Kenton County was established. Two years later the town of Kenton, Ohio, was founded. In 1849 the townspeople of Maysville, Simon's old Limestone, made arrangements for a new cemetery with a mound in the center which was to be Kenton's

End of the Trail

grave when their hero's body should be "brought back home."

In 1854 the Ohio Legislature appropriated $1000 for a monument to be erected over his grave after it was removed to "some suitable place."

Until the end of the Civil War, Ohio and Kentucky would squabble over where his final resting place would be. Finally in 1865 the Ohio Legislature got around to appropriating $5000 for a monument over his permanent resting place at Urbana. There his bones were reinterred and not again disturbed.

Doubtless Simon Kenton's fame would have equaled or surpassed Daniel Boone's if he had had a popular biography written during his lifetime, or soon thereafter. Nevertheless, few books about the border were written for fifty years after Kenton's death without a chapter or a sketch being devoted to his adventures. There were also several blood-and-thunder dime novels written using Simon Kenton as the hero.

Dr. Lyman Copeland Draper conceived the idea of doing Simon Kenton's biography, and he gathered quantities of notes by going directly to the people who were still living who had known the pioneer. He also gathered a voluminous correspondence from similar sources. However, Dr. Draper died before he got the book written.

Many years later William Hayden English discovered the Draper notes in the archives of the State Historical Society of Wisconsin and used the material for his *Conquest of the Country Northwest of the River Ohio*. Later

Frontier Hero

Theodore Roosevelt used the same sources of the Kenton material in his *Winning of the West*. But none of the writings about him achieved much popularity and so Simon Kenton, who lived history and made it and whose services to the westward movement are without equal, has been an unsung hero.

Bibliography

Beman, Irving. "Two Interesting Traditions," *Western History*, Vol. III, March 1886.
Brown, T. J. "Kenton's Chillicothes," *Ohio Archeological and Historical Quarterly*, Vol. XII, July 1903.
────── "Kenton's Gantlet at Chillicothe," *Ohio Archeological and Historical Quarterly*, Vol. XIII, October 1904.
Cattermole, E. G. *Famous Frontiersmen, Pioneers and Scouts*. Tarrytown, New York: W. Abbott, 1906.
Clark, Thomas D. *A History of Kentucky*. New York: Prentice-Hall, Inc., 1937.
Coleman, Robert T. "Simon Kenton," *Harper's Magazine*, Vol. XXVIII, February 1864.
Collins, Lewis and Richard. *The History of Kentucky*, Vol. II.
Ellett, Elizabeth Fries. *Pioneer Women of the West*. New York, 1852.
English, William Hayden. *The Conquest of the Country Northwest of the River Ohio*. Indianapolis, 1896.
Federal Writer's Project. New York: Harcourt, Brace & Co., 1954.
Frost, John. *Border Wars of the West*. Cincinnati, 1853.
Graham, Christopher C. "Simon Kenton," *Louisville Monthly Magazine*, Vol. I, March 1879.
Hartley, Cecil B. *Life and Adventures of Lewis Wetzel*. New York, 1860.
Howe, Henry. *Historical Collections of Ohio*. Cincinnati, 1847.
Johnston, C. H. L. *Famous Scouts*. Boston, 1910.
Kelsey, D. M. *Pioneer Heroes and Daring Deeds*. St. Louis, 1882.
Kenton, Edna. *Simon Kenton: His Life and Period*. Garden City: Doubleday, Doran, 1930.
McClung, John Alexander. *Sketches of Western Adventure*. Maysville, 1832.

Frontier Hero

McDonald, Donald John. *Biographical Sketches.* Cincinnati, 1838.
McFarland, Robert W. "Simon Kenton," *Ohio Archeological and Historical Quarterly*, Vol. XIII, April 1904.
McMeekin, Clark. *Old Kentucky Country.* New York, 1957.
Marshall, Humphrey. *History of Kentucky.* Frankfort, 1812.
Mowry, W. A. *American Pioneers.* New York, 1905.
Patrick, William. "Sketch of Simon Kenton," *History of Champaign County*, Ohio, 1872.
Roosevelt, Theodore. *The Winning of the West.* New York, 1889–1896.
Thomas, Frederick William. *Sketches of Character.* Louisville, 1849.
Willson, Annie E. "A Pioneer in His Corn-Patch," *American History Magazine*, Vol. XXIII, June 1890.

Index

Allegheny wilderness, 26
American War of Independence, 45, 47, 62, 65, 89
Americans, 89, 90, 91, 158, 160
arks, 115
Arrowsmith, John, 170
Arrowsmith, Mason, 170-71
Arrowsmith, Samuel, 62-63
Ashe, Thomas, 148-49
Auglaize River, 125

Bacon, Henry, 169
Bickley, John, 168
Big Grave Creek, 31
Big Sandy River, 32, 39, 42
Billy George, 135-36, 142-44
Black Fish, Chief, 65, 69
Black Snake, Chief, 117, 136
Blue Licks, 56-60, 115
Bonah, Chief, 138
Boone, Daniel, 60-61, 64, 65, 69-70, 73-74, 97, 108, 145-46, 167
Boone, Mrs., 145
Boonesborough, 60-61, 64, 69, 74, 97
Bowman, Colonel, 73
Bracken, Jesse, 144
British, 42-50, 62, 71-72, 86, 87, 88-91, 92, 96, 100, 158, 160-61

buffalo, 56, 60, 63
Bull Run Mountain, 13, 19
Bullock, Nathaniel, 92-95
Burnett, Judge Jacob, 129
Butler, Mr., 26
Butler, Simon. *See* Kenton, Simon

Cabin Creek, 51
Canada, 160, 161
Captina, 45
Cartwright, Samuel, 41
Champaign County, 155, 163
Cheat River, 26
Cheat Valley region, 25
Cherokee, 135, 142
Cherokee Fort, 72
Chillicothe, 74, 78, 178
Chi-ux-Ko, 139, 143
Cincinnati, Ohio, 128, 131, 176, 177
Clark, Abey, 140
Clark, George Rogers, 43-45, 46, 62-64, 68, 71-74, 77, 92, 95-97, 113, 165
Clark, Robert, 107, 108-09, 113
Coffer, Jesse, 92-95
Colonials, 90, 92. *See also* Americans
Congress, 139, 140

Index

Conquest of the Country Northwest of the River Ohio, 181
Coon, John, 138
Cornstalk, Chief, 48-49
Covington, 177
Cresap, Colonel, 46, 49
Crow, James, 175
Cummins, Ellen, 15-18; now Mrs. Leachman, 101
Cummins, Mr., 15
Cummins, Mrs., 15

Dayton, Ohio, 176
"debtor's law," 155, 168
Delaware, 31
Detroit, 89-93, 96
Donalson, Israel, 128
Dowden, Archibald, 133, 144
Dowden, John, 133
Dowden, Martha, 110-112. See also Kenton, Martha
Dowden, Mrs., 110-11
Draper, Dr. Lyman Copeland, 181
Drennan's Lick, 71
Druillard, George, 107
Druillard, Pierre, 88-90, 106-07
Dumfries, 13, 18-19
Duncan's Tavern, 50
Dunmore, Lord, 43, 45, 46, 48-50
Dunmore War, 45-49

Ecorse River, 91
Edgar, John, 92-93, 153-54
Edgar, Mrs., 92-93, 153
Elk River, 33, 47
Elkhorn River, 100, 129
English, William Hayden, 181

Fallen Timbers, battle of, 126
Fauquier County, Virginia, 19, 101

Felix, Trader, 135, 140
Finley, James, 105
Finley, Reverend Robert, 105
flatboats, 115
Fort Defiance, 125
Fort Greenville, 125
Fort Pitt, 27, 38, 43, 48, 50
Fort Recovery, 125
Fort Washington, 116
Fort Wayne, 149
France, 158
Frankfort, Kentucky, 171
French, 51, 88, 90

Galloway, Major James, 170, 175
Gano, Major General John S., 144
Georgia, 99
Ghent, Belgium, treaty at, 161
Gibson, John, 30
Girty, Simon, 44-45, 46, 48, 85-88
Graham, Mr., 19
Great Britain, 43, 158
Great Kanawha River, 33, 39
Greathouse, Jacob, 27, 41
Greenbriar County, 40
Greenville, 146, 149
Greenville, Treaty of, 126
Grille, William, 27, 41

Haggin, John, 64-65, 71
Hamilton, commander of British army at Detroit, 90, 92
Harrod, Captain, 64
Harrodsburg, 61, 62, 64, 65, 73, 96
Hinkston, John, 60, 100
Hinkston's Station, 61, 64-65

Ice's Ford, 26
Indiana, 140, 179
Indians, 27, 30-31, 35, 38, 39, 42-43, 45-50, 57-59, 62-65, 69-71,

[186]

Index

Indians—continued
74, 76-91, 92, 94, 96-97, 100, 104, 107, 108-09, 112-16, 117-19, 120-23, 126, 134-38, 140, 146, 149-51, 159. *See also* individual tribes
Ireland, 19

Jackson, President Andrew, 174
Jarboe, Elizabeth, 130-31. *See also* Kenton, Elizabeth
Jarboe, Stephen, 130
Johnson, Daniel, 26
Jones, Amos, 37-38
Jones, John Gabriel, 62-63
Jones, Martha, 37-38

Kanawha, 31
Kaskaskia, 72
Kelsey, Thomas, 115
Kenton, Benjamin (brother), 13, 101
Kenton County, 180
Kenton, Elizabeth "Betsey" (wife), 131, 133-34, 137, 139, 140, 165-66, 167-68, 174-75, 176, 177-80. *See also* Jarboe, Elizabeth
Kenton, Elizabeth (daughter), 140, 156, 166
Kenton, Frances (sister), 13, 101
Kenton, Jane (sister), 13, 101
Kenton, John (brother), 13-19, 126-27, 163, 168, 173
Kenton, John (son), 119, 130-31, 144-46, 153-54, 157
Kenton, Mark (father), 13-20, 101, 102
Kenton, Mark, Jr. (brother), 13-19, 98, 101
Kenton, Martha (wife), 112, 124, 130. *See also* Dowden, Martha

Kenton, Mary Miller (mother), 13, 101
Kenton, Mary (sister), 13, 101
Kenton, Mary (daughter), 141, 166
Kenton, Matilda (daughter), 131, 137, 166, 175, 179
Kenton, Nancy (sister), 13, 101, 112
Kenton, Nancy (daughter), 112, 119, 130-31, 166
Kenton, Ohio, 180
Kenton, Ruth Jane (daughter), 166
Kenton, Sarah (daughter), 126, 130-31
Kenton, Simon, his family, 13; helps in rolling, 14-19; at 15, 15; in love, 15; is hunter in family, 20-21; in fight, 22; thinks he committed murder, 23; runs away, 23; changes name, 26; in search of Kentucky cane lands, 28, 50-52; learns Indian language and ways, 30-32; makes camp, 33-34; is attacked by Indians, 35; escapes, 36-37; works as hunter, 39; longs to return home, 39, 40; guides explorers, 39-40, 62; meets George Rogers Clark, 43-44; enlists with British, 44; in war against Indians, 45-49; at 19, 46; friendship with Girty, 48; claims rights to land, 54-55; visits other settlements, 60-61; meets Daniel Boone, 61; is hunter for settlers, 65-66, 69, 71, 74; is appointed chief of scouts, 69, 73-74; rescues Boone, 70; in attacks against British, 71-72; captured by Indians, 77; is

Index

Kenton, Simon—continued
  tortured, 78-80, 81, 82; rain saves him from death, 83-84; is rescued by Girty, 85; is taken prisoner again, 87; is turned over to British, 90; is allowed to do as he pleases, 91; gets information about British, 92; escapes, 93-94; returns to Kentucky, 96; still dreams of land empire, 98; hears news of family, 98; is not a murderer, 98; goes back to using rightful name, 99; becomes one of largest landholders, 100-01; moves family to Kentucky, 102-03; death of father, 102; establishes station, 104; forms Kenton's Boys, 107-09, 112, 115-19; marriage, 112; children, 112, 119, 126, 131, 140, 141, 149, 156-57, 165-66; due to him northern Kentucky no longer wilderness, 116; is held in great awe by Indians, 117; his expedition against Tecumseh, 121-23; fights under Wayne, 125-26; his generosity, 127, 130; in legal battles over land, 129, 140, 152, 163; his wife dies, 130; remarries, 131; moves to Ohio, 131; involved in more Indian troubles, 135-38, 142-44; starts school, 138; loses his Ohio lands, 139; his Indian treaty invalid, 140-41; elected brigadier general, 144; buys land in Missouri, 145; averts Indian trouble, 147, 150-51; is robbed, 152-53; his earnings meager, 153; his stores fail, 154; character and description of, 155-56, 158; imprisoned for debt, 156, 167, 169; death of daughters, 156, 166; lives in Urbana, 157; fights in War of 1812, at 58, 160; writes reminiscences, 165; sells land to pay debts, 166; authorizes writing of his biography, 168; at 69, 169; is given back Kentucky lands, 172; death of brother John, 173; is given pension, 174; arranges fifty-year reunion, 175, 177; attends last camp meeting, 178; his mind begins to fail, 179; death of, 180; in memory of, 180-82

Kenton, Simon, Jr. (son), 126, 130-31, 165-66

Kenton, Thomas (nephew), 140, 146

Kenton, William (brother), 19-20, 126-27, 140

Kenton, William Miller (son), 140, 149, 166, 168, 174, 179

"Kenton's Boys," 107-08, 112, 115-19, 120, 121-23, 125-26, 133

Kenton's Station, 104-07, 109, 112, 115, 123

Kenton's Trace, 133, 139-40, 153

Kentucky, 28, 32, 50, 52-54, 57, 60-62, 64, 90, 96, 98-99, 100-31, 138, 140, 152, 154, 155, 167-68, 169, 170-73, 175-76, 181

Kentucky River, 54

Kinsualla, John, 107, 113

Lagonda Creek, 139, 142, 149, 152, 156

Laurel Creek, Pennsylvania, 139

Lawrence River, 62

Leachman, Mr., 21-22

Index

Leachman, William, 15-18, 22-23, 98, 101
Lernoult, Captain, 90-92
Letart's Falls, 32, 51
Lewis, Captain, 47-49
Lewiston, 159
Lexington, Kentucky, 98-99
Licking River, 96, 97
Limestone, 108, 112, 115, 116, 120, 176
Limestone Creek, 51-52, 100; Kenton's station at, 104, 106-07
Limestone Treaty, the, 113
Little Miami River, 121
Little Kanawha River, 39
Livingston, James, 117-19
Lock, Joseph, 41
Logstown, 30
Logan, Benjamin, 108
Logan, Captain, 64
Logan, Chief, 30, 42-43, 49-50, 88
Logan's Gap, 108
Logan's Station, 74
Louisiana Purchase, 144, 146
Lowther's Fort, 47
Luce, Zephaniah, 164

McCarty, William, 154
McClelland's Station, 61, 63
McClung, John Alexander, 168
McConnell, Mr., 129, 167
McCulloch, Mr., 48
McDonald, John, 168
McDonald's campaign, 45-46
McIlvane, Charles, 147
McMahon, "Wild Man," 125-26
McPherson, Captain James, 146-47, 149-50
Machachak, 108
Mad River, 146; settlement at, 148-49
Mad Valley, 149
Madrid, 145
Mahon, Joe, 27, 38, 41
Mahon, John, 27, 38, 41
Manchester, 120
Martin's Station, 96
Maryland, 130
Mason County, Kentucky, 54, 116-17, 123, 167, 172
Massie, Nathaniel, 120
May, John, 117
May's Lick, 118
Maysville, Kentucky, 104, 180
Miami River, 140, 159
Mingoes, 30-31, 42-43, 49
Mississippi River, 71, 145, 157
Missouri, 131, 144-46, 154, 157, 163
Moluntha's Town, 108
Monongahela River, 26, 27, 28, 47, 102, 139
Montgomery, Alexander, 74, 77
Moore, Major, 150
Muskingum Indians, 45-46
Muskingum River, 46

Napoleon, 158
New Jersey, 26
Newmarket, 139
Newport, 177
Nip and Tuck, 61

Ohio, 45, 101, 131, 133-56, 163, 169, 173, 175, 177-78, 181
Ohio River, 30, 32, 34, 39, 50, 71, 74-75, 93, 95, 102, 114, 117, 118, 121, 125
Old Fort Washington, 175, 177
One Eye, 136-37
Ottoway Town, 136
Owen, Jinney, 135
Owen, William, 134-35

[189]

Index

Paint Creek, 71
Parkison, John, 170
Pennsylvania, 128, 139
Pickett, Thomas, 168
Piqua, 97
Pittsburgh, 128, 139
"planting possession" of land, 54
Point Pleasant, battle of, 47, 49
Prophet, the, 149
Provence settlement, 27

Record, Spencer, 114
Redstone Old Fort, 139
Reed, James, 149
Reese, Joel, 38-39
Renick, Robert, 144
Revolutionary War, 45, 47, 62, 65, 89
Reynolds, Joseph, 147
Riddle's Station, 61, 96
Robinson, James, 152
"rolling," 13
Roosevelt, Theodore, 182

St. Charles, Missouri, 145, 153, 157
St. Louis, Missouri, 154, 157
Salt River, Kenton's Station at, 102-04
Sandusky River, 87-88
Scioto, 88
Scott, General, 120
Senecas, 48
Shawnee, 30, 49, 65, 69-71, 81, 112-14, 118-19, 146-47, 166
Shelby, Governor, 160
Sketches of Western Adventure, 168, 176
Smith, David, 169
Solomon's Town, 159
"Spanish grant," 154-55

Springfield, Ohio, 133, 139, 156, 178
Spy Buck, 138-39
Stoner, Michael, 60
Stony Creek, 137, 146
Strader, George, 27-39, 50

Tecumseh, 121-23, 140, 146, 150-51, 160
Three Islands, 39, 63, 120
Todd, Colonel Robert, 112
"tomahawk rights" to land, 55

United States, 158, 161
Urbana, 146, 155-59, 160, 164, 169, 181

Virginia, 13, 19, 39, 43, 62, 64, 65, 71, 99

Wabash Indians, 140
Wabash River, 140
Wapatomika, 81-82, 86, 146
War of 1812, 158-61
Ward, James, 172
Ward, William, 149-50, 162-63
Warm Springs, 26
Washburn, Cornelius, 121-22
Washington, Kentucky, 101, 104-05, 113, 127, 140, 176
Watkins, Captain, 71
Wayne, General Anthony, 124-26
Western Christian Advocate, 168
Western Spy, the, 144
Wheeling, 45, 128
Whiteman, Benjamin, 150, 171
Whittlesey, Trader, 135-36
Williams, Thomas, 50-63, 167
Winning of the West, 182
Wisconsin State Historical Society, 181

[190]

Index

Wolf, Chief, 135-36
Wood, Dr. John, 39-40
Wood, Reverend William, 105, 112
Woods, Tobias, 114
Worthington, William, 168

Xenia, Ohio, 177-78
Yaeger, John, 27-36
Yellow Creek, 30, 35
Zane's Trace, 128
Zanesfield, 166, 174

About the Author

SHANNON GARST was born in Ironwood, Michigan, on July 24, 1899 and moved to Denver, Colorado, at the age of four, where she received most of her schooling. At the age of seventeen she went to Hood River, Oregon, where she taught school for four years. She now lives in Wyoming. Her first acceptances in the field of writing were stories she did for her own children. Since then she has become a versatile writer of juvenile fiction and biography.

DATE DUE

92
K 19 **Garst, Shannon**
Frontier hero

DATE DUE	BORROWER'S NAME	
NOV 21 1972	Briskey	8
3/9/73	O. McNally	4
APR 20 1973	R. Horvath	4
MAY 4 1973	P. Horvath	4

92
K 19   **Garst, Shannon**
Frontier hero

Please return to:
Aquinas Academy Library
2308 West Hardies Road
Gibsonia, PA 15044
724-444-0722

DISCARD

B 6-488